#MEGADEALS™

JOHAN ABERG CHRISTOPHER ENGMAN

Edited and proofread by Cole Ruth and Paul Redstone
Research provided by Tonya S. Pixton, PhD, in cooperation with the two authors
Illustrations by Josefin Herolf
Designed by Tomas Ring
Art direction and identity by Lina Földessy and Frida Jansson
Project management by Ulrika Carmine
Printed by Bulls Graphics AB

Second printing edition 2020.
ISBN: 978-91-985572-1-3

Megadeals Research AB
www.megadealsresearch.com

TABLE OF CONTENTS

INTRODUCTION

WHY ARE MEGADEALS A MEGA DEAL?

In the B2B world, the people bringing the largest deals to the table are often heroes with tremendous formal or informal power. This is because many of the biggest B2B organizations in the world have more than 80% of the total revenue coming from less than 1% of the customer base - often fewer than 100 customers. When you break down these numbers, you see that a few megadeals make up a large proportion of the 80%.

Since boards and management teams are concerned that this could be seen as a risk by investors, these revenue concentrations are often hidden from the outside world. But what if we look at it from another angle? What if most of the largest companies in the world actually became that large because they were able to master and win megadeals? If you are a megadealer or aspiring megadealer, it is worth knowing that many top megadealers have annual compensation packages exceeding

1 MUSD. It is likely that we will see the same annual compensation development for megadeal marketers.

There are no other books about megadeals

Very little has been written on megadeals, either from a sales perspective or a marketing perspective. In the world of sales, deal sizes are trending larger on one end of the spectrum, and smaller on the other. As deal sizes get smaller, there is a move from traditional selling to automated selling. But as the deals get larger, we are seeing an increase in complexity and the number of complex deals. See the illustration below.

MODIFIED VERSION OF PROSALES BUYING LOGIC MODEL*

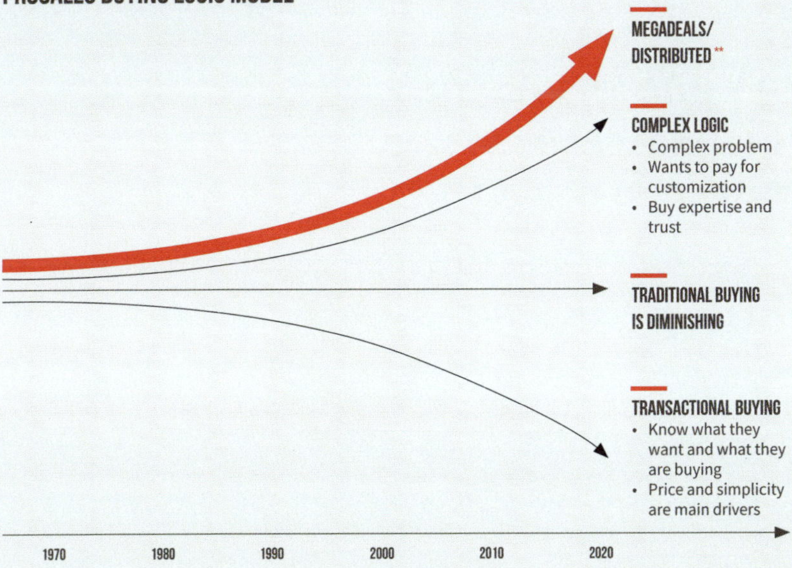

* Adapted from ProSales' Buying Logic Model by Henrik Larsson-Broman, Peter Siljerud, and Markus Ejenäs, "Supertrends - Future-proof Your Sales and Marketing," ProSales Institute (Stockholm, 2018).

** What Prosales calls "Distributed Selling" we call megadeals. Complex selling is becoming more complex and traditional selling is becoming more automated.

A megadeal has four core attributes:

1. The deal is valued at 10 MUSD or more (the biggest one we have seen was 15 BUSD).
2. There is high to ultra-high complexity in the deal (complexity here does not refer only to the complexity of the solution, which is often written about in sales books, but more about this later).
3. The deal includes change management.
4. The deal often contains a mix of hardware, software and services.

Complex B2B selling is too broad a term

When studying what fits under the umbrella of "complex B2B selling," you'll find a broad spectrum of deals. They are all called complex B2B deals.

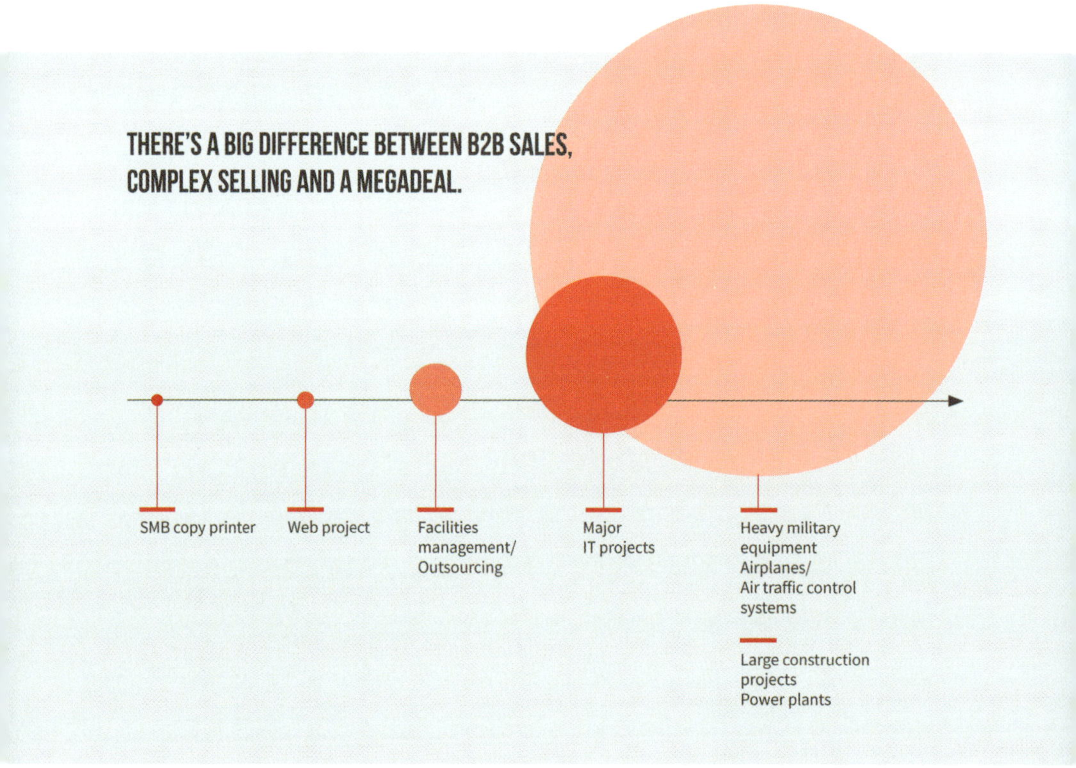

THERE'S A BIG DIFFERENCE BETWEEN B2B SALES, COMPLEX SELLING AND A MEGADEAL.

Examples of companies that make megadeals are: IBM, SAP, GE, SAAB, Lockheed Martin, Airbus, Skanska, Ericsson, Accenture, Tata Consulting Services and Siemens, to name just a few.

Managing a megadeal is not the same as complex selling

We believe megadeals should be considered independently from complex selling because of four aspects that will significantly affect your sales and marketing approach. Other books on sales and marketing do not address these five aspects:

1. Megadeals often require six months to a year of work by a dedicated cross-functional team. In short, there is too much money on the line to fail. Pursuing a megadeal is therefore not a process of qualifying leads so much as disqualifying them.
2. If your offer does not align with your customer's key initiatives, it is almost impossible to find the money for your megadeal. (We address this in Chapter 1.)
3. If you cannot understand or influence the ecosystem around the deal, you will not close the deal. In most cases there are more than 100 relevant stakeholders. For many reasons this represents a really tricky part of forging a megadeal. (We cover this in Chapters 2, 3 and 4.)
4. Megadeals per definition involve a lot of risks. Being able to control and mitigate those risks, rather than just maximizing the upside, is a key capability - one that is barely discussed in sales and marketing literature. (We address this in Chapter 5.)
5. In the megadeals space, marketing is often derided for not contributing significant business value. Yet this is far from the truth. We cover this in detail in part two of the book.

Most megadeals are made with large organizations where large sums of money are usually allocated to key initiatives or strategic programs. Megadeals are almost exclusively made in contexts where the buyer is not a handful of people, but many departments, countries, levels of hierarchy and even external organizations. In other words, there are often more than 100 people involved. To navigate, influence and move an entire ecosystem, you need a strong toolbox of methods and skills for marketing and sales. It is critical that you always have enough intelligence about the deal. When large amounts of money and major company changes are on the table, obtaining a low-risk deal is more important than a low price or an aggressive upside.

Common sense is not common practice

We know that everyone who studies this book (including seasoned megadealers) will walk away with two or three insights that will transform their business if implemented.

But... we also know that common sense is not common practice and that people do not always act on what they know. In that case, everyone would have great, loving, intimate relationships, and be perfectly fit - and we know that the majority of people aren't, so it isn't!

So instead of asking yourself the question, "Do I know this?" ask yourself:

- Have I personally mastered this and can I execute consistently on a high level?
- Has my team mastered this and can they execute consistently on a high level?
- Has our company mastered this and can it execute consistently on a high level?

We also recommend that you not just read this book, but rather study it and reflect on its implications for your business, both short and long-term. It is an actionable guide that is created for execution. If you don't execute, you won't get the value out of it. If it is difficult for you to get your team to study the book, you can also buy a management summary by the authors, both in written and video format. Live webinars are also available.

This book has three parts:

1. An overview of the five cornerstones that are required to close megadeals.

2. Megadeal marketing and sales tools and capabilities that a stellar megadealer team needs to master and execute to gain a competitive edge. This includes, for example, a summary of the foundations of normal B2B complex selling, megadeal account-based marketing and enterprise social selling.
3. Megadeal complexities. Complex deals are often described as having many stakeholders, long sales cycles, and high perceived risk. This is an unfortunate simplification because there are six additional complexities to take into account. Entire books could be written about these complexities, but we asked experts in two of them to

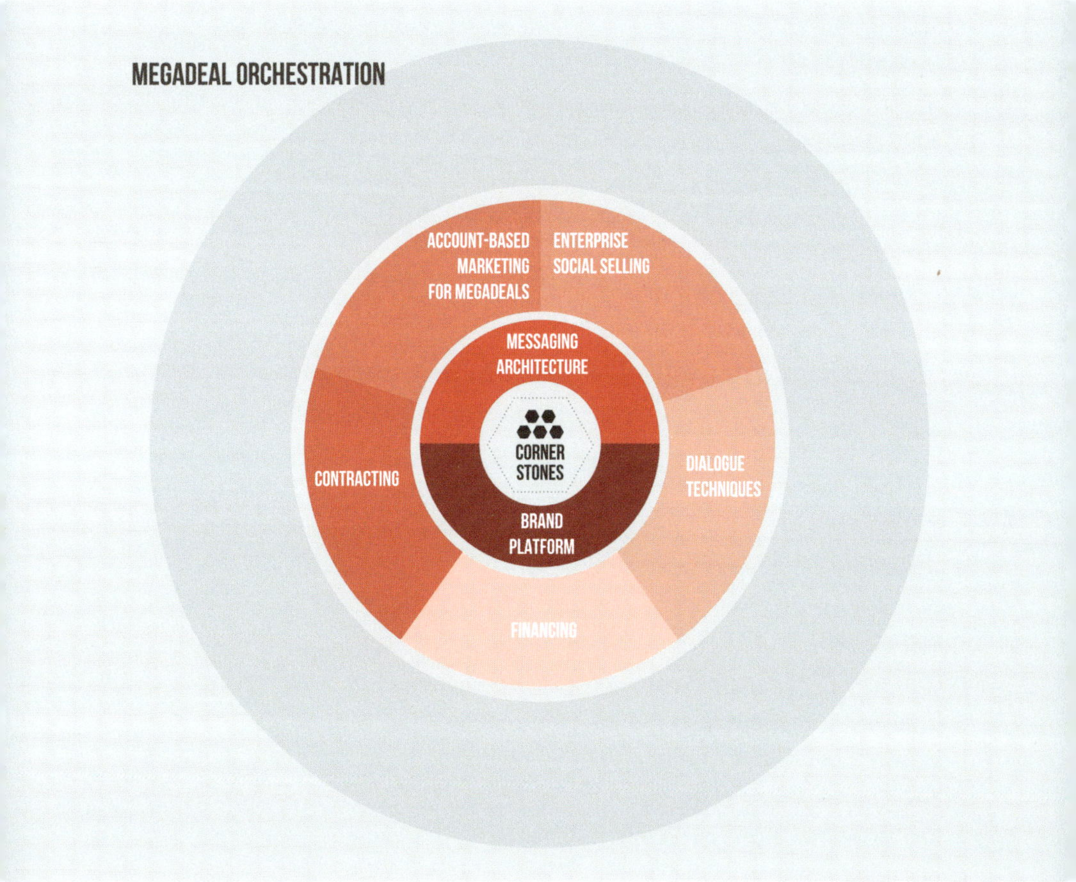

provide insights into their respective subjects. We are very grateful to Alexander Helling of Baseload Capital for his introduction to the three most common financing structures in megadeals, as well as to David Frydlinger of Cirio and Kate Vitasek, founder of Vested, for their chapter on relational contracting, which we believe is an ideal fit for many megadeals.

About the authors

Johan Aberg and Christopher Engman have worked with 100+ Fortune 500 companies whose marketing and sales are focused on large deals. Both frequently speak about megadeals and related areas such as account-based marketing, enterprise social selling and automated marketing mix modeling.

Methodology

1. Based on work with sales and marketing people in 100+ Fortune 500 companies and their largest deals, we created a set of hypotheses.
2. More than 60 megadealers participated in 2 to 10 hours of interviews in which we presented our hypotheses and asked for feedback. Each megadealer suggested what he or she would add or remove from the hypotheses.
3. Adjustments were made on an ongoing basis according to the valuable input we received, making it possible to present an improved version in the subsequent interview.
4. In each part of the book, we identify and outline the best strategies of the best megadealers.

The megadeals domain is so complex that it would be impossible for us to map out every aspect of it in this book. That would be like trying to detail every system required for a mission to Mars. That said, we applied a method to a large enough group of respondents to say that our claims are scientifically proven. However, as practitioners of knowledge in 21st century, we see this book as a means rather than an end. Our intent is to open the electronic version of this book up for crowdsourcing of a sort, so that in future releases our glasses will be even sharper, and our scope wider, enabling us and others to see the megadeal ecosystem more clearly. Here's how it will work: we'll keep track of your suggestions, examples, stories and critiques. If we publish your contribution, we will reference you (i.e., you will be named in future editions of the book).

01 +100 FORTUNE 500 COMPANIES

02 HYPOTHESES AND FRAMEWORK

03 60+ DEEP INTERVIEWS

04 ITERATIVE IMPROVEMENTS

05 BEST OF THE BEST

Some areas not covered in this book

Becoming an expert at megadeals is not only about sales and marketing. There are several other key components to take into account. To go deep, this book is mainly focused on the sales and marketing aspects of megadeals. Some areas that are worth considering, but which are outside the scope of this book, include: How to build the megadeal organization, megadeal growth hacking, trade compliance, how smaller companies can transition to making megadeals, how to manage megadeal salespeople, and KPIs for megadeals.

Who should read this book?

Through our research, we have found that most megadealers excel at a few of the areas in the book - at least a few each (or they wouldn't be megadealers). They are always lacking in at least one or two areas, or need improvement. Megadealers are very ambitious, so filling gaps in their toolbox is something they will do. This is why they are winning. If you are doing more conventional complex selling with deal sizes under 10 MUSD, and with medium complexity, you might want to join the big league of selling. The same is also true for marketers: a few of the areas are mastered by each person, but a few are still to be mastered. For aspiring megadeal marketers, understanding and learning about megadeals (both the marketing and the sales aspects) is critical for a career involving the biggest money in the business world. CEOs, CMOs and CSOs should also read this book to be able to implement part or all of its content. People outside the world of megadeals who read this book will get a fascinating look at where the big money is, and a sense of the scale and complexity of the changes taking place in business today.

A new way to create practical advice with a scientific approach

We have received feedback both from megadealers and others throughout the research and writing of the book. The subject is complex partly because megadeals are complex, partly because sales and marketing are transforming quickly, and partly because being a master at megadeals requires a strong competitive edge. We are digital at heart, and because of that, we wanted to create a new approach for this book. The approach consists of two parts:

1. You will find tools, videos and workshop material online. The purpose is to give you inspiration and support in key areas so that you can quickly excel at making megadeals.
2. As you read the book, please send any insights, stories, additions, suggested deletions, etc., to hello@megadealsresearch.com
   If your input makes sense, we will include it in the next release of the book and note the source. We believe in the wisdom of the crowd.

Why did we write this book?

For most enterprise B2B companies, megadeals are the key drivers to success and growth. Yet within Fortune 500 companies, only a few know how megadeals are made.

We are sales, marketing, and psychology nerds who have thought about megadeals 24/7 for the past 10-15 years, and we strive to be the global center of excellence for megadeals.

There are four main drivers behind our motivation to create this book and master the subject (all were equally important):

- Being able to share this knowledge with large and/or high-growth companies to help them master megadeals is a big inspiration.
- We have a personal interest in investing in megadeals and potential megadeal companies, and being able to add extraordinary value for growth.
- We want to help companies that have a true and strong "why" to make the world better and improve millions of lives.
- To create a strong and intimate network of the best of the best in order to help grow those B2B businesses who sell mainly to a few large customers.

As megadeals are not covered in any sales and marketing literature, we are grateful for the opportunity this has created. Growth hacking, sales, social selling, ABM and marketing literature exist in abundance for simpler sales. It is a great privilege to be able to define a segment that is so important for most B2B companies.

Is marketing really important for megadeals?

The simple answer is yes. But let us explain why. Unfortunately, in some megadeal companies, marketing has a low perceived value or is seen as an event function and not as a key to protecting existing customers, winning new megadeal customers or growing existing megadeal customers.

Marketing can become an important competitive advantage or

disadvantage depending on the level of the marketing department's capabilities and authority.

Technology has changed how large organizations make really important decisions:

- Internal transparency is greater than ever, and penetrates deeper into organizations, increasing the negative consequences of making the wrong decision.
- Today, more people are involved in these decisions. In one case, a record number of 499 people had to sign an NDA on the selling side.

Megadeals also involve a lot of money and a lot of organizational change. Megadeal marketing can, at scale, provide straightforward executable principles that will support:

1. The establishment of trust by lowering the perceived risks of the deal.
2. The creation of consensus at scale around the major challenges, what type of solution is needed and what vendor would be the best fit.

We know for a fact (because of direct involvement) about deals larger than 100 MUSD that started completely on LinkedIn via social selling.

What drives megadealers and why aspire to that level?

It is not difficult to be among the top 1%. The tools in this book, when studied one by one, can be learned and mastered.

As mentioned, many megadealers have great formal or informal power because their work makes a huge impact on the companies they represent, and on their customers and the end customer. If you are in sales or marketing and you want to make a big impact, then the world of megadeals is where you want to be.

Many megadealers make more than 1 MUSD per year. When you are responsible for bringing in the largest amounts of money to your company, compensation is no longer a tough discussion. The biggest accumulated sales commission we came across in our interviews was 47 MUSD.

Furthermore, because of their size, scope, complexity and status, megadeals are deeply meaningful to the megadealers behind them. They present an opportunity to change the world for the better on a massive scale.

PART I

MEGADEAL CORNERSTONES

CHAPTER 1

KEY INITIATIVES

If you want to win a megadeal, understanding and applying the contents of this chapter is one of the easiest cornerstones you can put into place.

All large companies have a few top priorities, goals and strategies that they use to drive change within the company. In different companies, they are called different things, such as key initiatives, strategic priorities, strategic programs, strategic initiatives, big bets, etc. In our framework, we call them key initiatives.

Key initiatives are the means through which a business's vision is translated into practice by overcoming the most important problems and issues; they are kernels of the business strategy. Key initiatives are collections of finite-duration discretionary projects and programs outside of the organization's day-to-day operational activities that are designed to help the organization achieve long-term targeted performance and stay relevant and successful over time. A key initiative typically has a time frame of 1-10 years (often only 3-5 years) and should be specific enough that it can be measured. There should be no doubt whether a

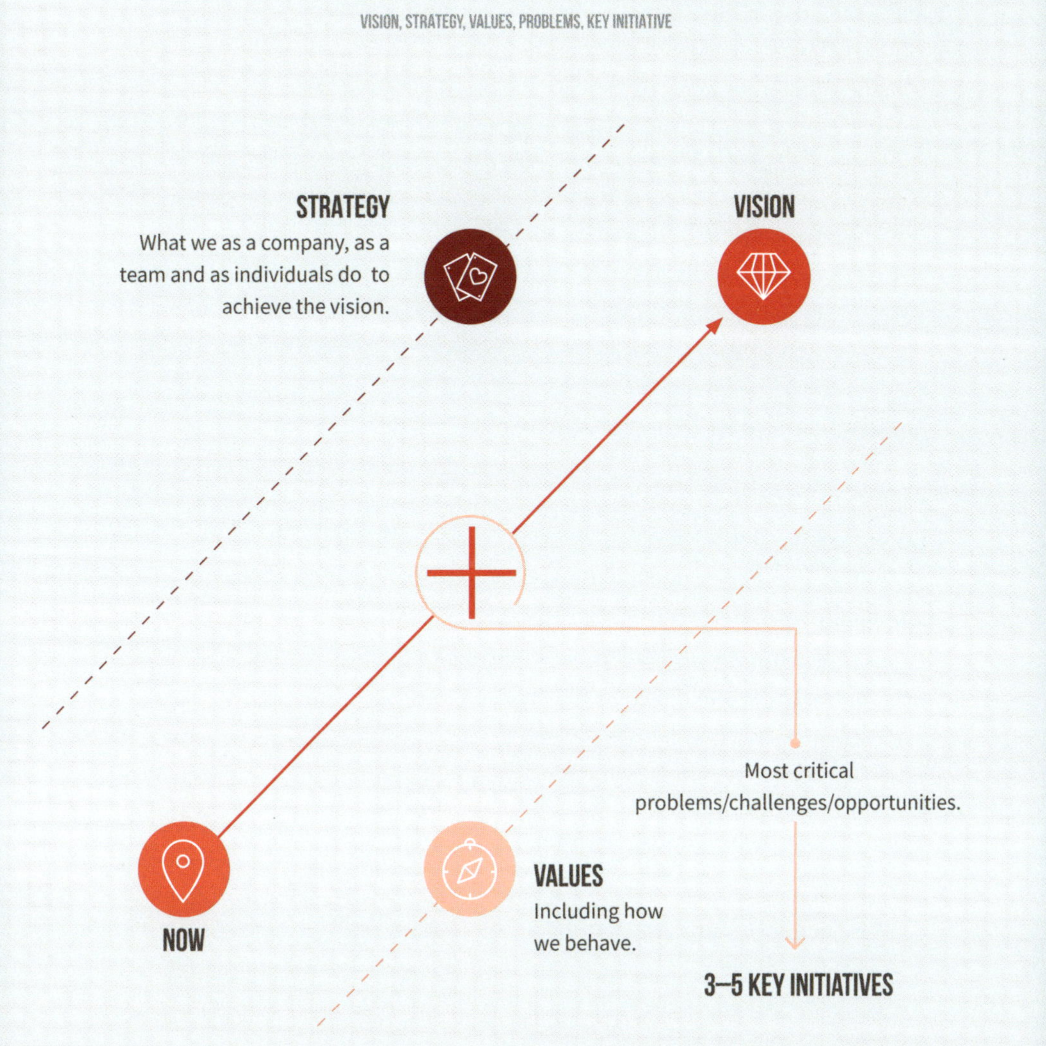
VISION, STRATEGY, VALUES, PROBLEMS, KEY INITIATIVE
STRATEGY
What we as a company, as a team and as individuals do to achieve the vision.
VISION
Most critical problems/challenges/opportunities.
NOW
VALUES
Including how we behave.
3–5 KEY INITIATIVES

given key initiative has been successful or not. They also tend to have clear deadlines, which is why great key initiatives are formulated, "from X to Y by when." Conversely, some are not formulated this clearly, probably due to a fear of accountability.

One megadealer we know, we'll call him Tom, was once thrown into a meeting with an important customer at the last minute and told he had just 20 minutes to contribute. For most of the meeting, his colleagues described how their software worked. At the end of the meeting, as the clock ticked down, Tom could tell the customer was not convinced. With just a few minutes left, he made the case for how the customer could use the software to accelerate the delivery rate in their organization. Suddenly, all 15 people from their management team stood up and said, "This is what we want!"

"I made a lucky guess," Tom recalled. It turned out that his customer had a key initiative focused on accelerating throughput - and it had been going on for a while. "Of course, had I known more about the customer and been working in that area, I would have known what mattered to them and we would have closed that deal faster," Tom concluded.

There is an old saying that a good goalkeeper has a lot of luck. Read on. This chapter is all about making you a better goalkeeper.

How to recognize a key initiative when you see one

Many sales organizations fail to understand the importance of key initiatives, and deals are lost because of the lack of understanding of how this works internally in the buying organization.

Megadeals involve large sums of money and often entail significant changes. If you want to know where large sums of money are being exchanged, and where significant changes are taking place in an organization, you will almost always find them among the key initiatives.

To extract mega money, you need to ensure that you are spending time with those clients for whom your offering matches one or many key initiatives. If you don't, you run a significant risk of meeting enthusiastic people on the client side, but ultimately see test budgets or small pilots at best. You will also have unbalanced marketing and sales costs since selling these pilots can take as long as closing a megadeal, and therefore drive up your costs. Don't get us wrong, you may often be laying important groundwork for a future megadeal in the process (when your offering eventually aligns with a newly established key initiative), but that deal is likely many years away. Therefore, the majority of your time should be spent with organizations for whom your offering could be the solution to an established key initiative. It doesn't need to be stated that they will buy a solution/service like yours, but you need to be able to clearly see how your offering fits into one of your client's key initiatives.

In transactional sales and complex selling, the lead qualification process looks like a funnel. Because it's not very expensive to pursue leads, your sales and marketing team can afford to cast a wide net.

SALES FUNNEL SHAPE

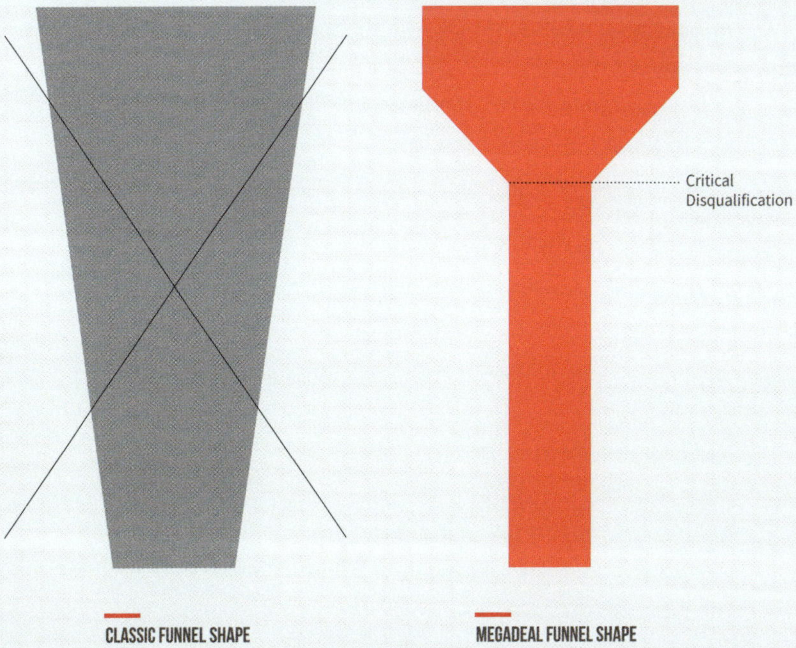

At worst it may cost you a few hours in meetings. Not so in a megadeal. We know of one company who spent 35 million USD in pursuit of a single deal. Because of the substantial investment in staffing and the length of time required to sign the contract, you cannot bet on ten potential customers at the same time. For this reason, the pursuit of a megadeal should start with disqualification rather than qualification. Where there once was a V-shaped funnel, you should now start seeing a T. Identifying how your offering solves a key intitiative of your customer is the first stage in the disqualification process.

Key initiatives are often cross-functional and focus on the major drivers in large businesses, such as:

- Growth
- Profitability
- Quality
- Sustainability
- Innovation
- People

We have listed examples of key initiatives below. We understand that you will get the point after the first few, but having the list in the back of your mind will help you recognize them when they are not explicitly stated. As it is extremely important to connect what you are selling to the customer's key initiatives, this list will also be useful for inspiration and discussion.

Examples of key initiatives:

1. Reach the targets in the Paris Agreement (such as reducing CO_2 emissions)
2. Increase product quality and decrease the number of failed products
3. Increase customer loyalty
4. Diversify the product portfolio
5. Diversify the customer base

6. Change the energy mix
7. Increase revenue and profitability from the core business
8. Digitalize the customer's buying journey
9. Increase the profitability and loyalty of global accounts
10. Increase the customer's lifetime value
11. Innovate away from a declining market/business area
12. Acquire companies that have made innovations in the coming or more recent paradigms
13. Make cost cuts to increase margins
14. Rewrite the code base of the main software product
15. Change the company's business model from CAPEX-heavy to OPEX-heavy (more recurring revenues)
16. Scale up production
17. Increase the organic growth rate
18. Increase cross-selling, selling more of the portfolio to the same customers
19. Increase market share in a specific market segment
20. Increase share of wallet in top 15 global accounts
21. Provide the best service in the industry
22. Grow percentage of sales from new products
23. Reduce pollution
24. Reduce energy consumption
25. Diversify the workforce
26. Consolidate acquisitions in terms of customers, processes, and culture
27. Improve employee retention
28. Increase the number of A-players in the organization

If you come across relevant key initiatives that you think should be on the list, please send them to: hello@megadealsresearch.com

The "low priority" trap

What you're selling may very likely solve clear issues for the buyer, so you might even find it odd that they don't respond faster when your offering is so obviously good for them. "They don't understand what is in their own best interests," you may find yourself saying.

In this case, it is very likely that your offering is low on the list of priorities. When companies go about setting key initiatives, a tough battle often ensues over which initiatives are the most important. After all, a company can only address so many initiatives at one time. Not all initiatives make the cut. If you have identified a problem for the buyer, but it didn't make it onto their list of key initiatives, you will hear comments such as, "This solves a real issue for us, but can we talk again after the summer - or next year? We have a few things that we need to sort out first in the short term."

Make a list of your customer's key initiatives and attempt to rank them if they have not done so. If the issue your offering can solve does not make the top four, you are barking up the wrong tree.

THE LOW PRIORITY TRAP

Example of what a company's list of key initiatives might look like:

KI 1	Digitalize
KI 2	Reduce pollution
KI 3	NPS x to NPS y
KI 4	Reduce costs by x%
…	
…	
…	
…	
	A low-priority issue that your offering can solve

This illustrates why it is so important to direct the focus and resources of your sales and marketing towards those customers for whom your offering will help solve a key initiative.

It is important to understand that when selling to most large companies, you are not only going up against other competitors but, even more importantly, against other initiatives.

How do you find out what an organization's key initiatives are?

Before looking for key initiatives, you and your team/colleagues should run an exercise where you agree on what type of key initiatives you would normally fall under. At author Christopher Engman's former company, Climeon, they learned that very few organizations would spend mega money on a heat power plant unless becoming greener was a key initiative for them. The sales team therefore decided not to spend time with potential customers unless this was in place.

If you sell some kind of outsourcing solution you could, for example, look for strategic initiatives that mention "core business." If "focus on the core business" is a key initiative, then an offer of outsourcing could be well timed. What kind of key initiatives have your customers had that impacted the last few large deals your organization has made?

Some organizations' key initiatives are easier to identify than others. Many listed companies have their key initiatives clearly described in their annual reports, mentioned in quarterly reports, and sometimes even referenced in press releases.

Annual reports

In many annual reports, you will find the initiatives spelled out, or at least it is possible to find clear clues about them.

The target organization's website and news flow

Key initiatives are a big part of a company's development and are therefore often mentioned (sometimes indirectly) in press releases and other corporate communication. When CEOs or other high-profile leaders are interviewed, key initiatives are often mentioned - not least because they are top of mind for those individuals.

Hard to find?

As mentioned, in some cases the key initiatives are hard to find. Some companies hide them because they do not want the competition to know what they are focusing on. If this is the case, the three methods above will not work well enough.

Low-level interviews/research calls

One way to identify a potential customer's key initiatives when they are not explicitly stated is by interviewing lower-level staff in the organization. Because executing key initiatives throughout an organization often requires the management to over-communicate internally, it is pretty easy to find out about them early on in your sales process. The drawback of using low-level interviews early on, however, when you really want to qualify or disqualify the target organization from your megadeal radar, is that they are significantly more time consuming than the other methods mentioned above. That said, most of the time, you will have enough information after interviewing 1-3 people to discern what the key initiatives are.

Industry initiatives

Sometimes an entire industry can share a specific key initiative. Often, this will be due to compliance, such as new laws and regulations (emissions levels, chip and pin, etc.), but it could also be related to a new technical trend (as a service vs. on-premise, smartphones overtaking traditional mobile phones, 5G, etc.). In this case, your potential customer may end up quickly establishing a key initiative in order to stay competitive or comply with a coming or anticipated new law or regulation.

For example, the International Maritime Organization has announced that penalties will apply to those companies that do not lower sulfur emissions to a certain level before the end of 2020. This has naturally had an affect on every company in the cruise and container shipping industry. For the fashion industry, there are many sustainable initiatives, such as the Better Cotton Initiative (BCI). In many countries, credit and debit card companies and banks have demanded that retailers standardize chips and pin codes, forcing retailers to make this a top priority. Airlines for America (A4A) and its members are part of a worldwide aviation coalition that has committed to a global framework on aviation and climate change under the United Nations body that sets standards and recommended practices for international aviation, the International Civil Aviation Organization (ICAO). The "global sectoral approach" for aviation carbon dioxide (CO_2) emissions includes an aggressive set of measures and emissions targets. In other words, you might not have to look far to find an industry initiative that is affecting your customer. By always keeping track of your target industry's big trends, you will be able to spot these waves of key initiatives and set your sales organization up to make multiple megadeals with a great amount of reuse between cases.

What options do I have if my offer is not part of a key initiative?
In our research, we have seen that trying to affect key initiatives within large enterprises is difficult and in many cases impossible.

So first off, if you want to make megadeals on a regular basis, it is critical that you spend your time wisely. We recommend spending less than 10% of your time to "market and sell" to clients that have no clear key initiatives connected to your offering. Social selling, covered in Chapter 8, is a great tool that you can work with early on in the sales cycle to attract attention before you begin a costly sales project.

Second, if your offer is relevant to your target customers' key initiatives, but you often have a hard time connecting your offer to those initiatives, you will need to repackage and/or innovate the product, service, and/or solution to make it relevant. Remember to think of key initiatives as the first step in disqualifying the wrong customers. When the mere pursuit of a megadeal can cost millions of dollars, you cannot afford to take on ten different potential customers. When you go for the win, you want to make sure that the conditions are in your favor.

EXERCISE

How well do you use key initiatives in the sales and marketing process? Run through these questions and apply them to your current prospective customers.

Step 1. What are the 3-7 key initiatives of organization x?

Make sure that you understand all the key initiatives, even ones that are not relevant to you. This will ensure that, when you interact with the customer, you will be seen as being "in the know." This will also enable you to better craft your offering to fit the buyer.

Step 2. Which key initiative(s) can you tie into?

Analyze and understand which key initiative(s) your offering ties into. Note that your offering doesn't have to be named in a key initiative. But you will need a clear description of why it fits.

Step 3. Who is leading the key initiative?

Identify the responsible people for each initiative. This is often covered in annual reports alongside a description of the initiative. Alternatively, it can be found by speaking with lower-level employees in the customer's organization.

Step 4. How is the key initiative measured and rewarded?

Because of the major importance of key initiatives in driving business transformation, they are often measured and rewarded in specific ways. Understanding how the customer measures and rewards success is critical to structuring your offering and message in the right way. It will help you set up the right business case, and give you insight into how you can reduce the buyer's risk.

Step 5. Which part of the organization is most affected by the key initiative?

Even though a key initiative indicates that an organization is focused on changing that aspect of its business, it might not affect the entire organization. However, these types of large-scale changes are often cross-functional, or include a few functions. Make sure that your team understands which areas of the customer's organization will be significantly affected.

Step 6. Why is your offering critical for the success of the key initiative?

If you want to tie your offering to the key initiative in a sticky way, make sure your offering is a critical factor for making the initiative a success. If there are many ways to achieve success with the initiative, it will weaken your competitive advantage. Perform a deep analysis of why your way of reaching success is better than other ways, and why you are better than other vendors. See the chapter on messaging architecture to obtain deeper insight on this.

KEY TAKEAWAYS

1. A megadeal is close to impossible to make if the buying organization does not have a key initiative that matches what you sell, so use this as an early qualifier/disqualifier.
2. Key initiatives are often found and described in annual reports, on the buying organization's website, and in its news flow.
3. Run an exercise internally about key initiatives and how they are important to your megadeals. List the most important initiatives that you have seen that match your offering.
4. Look for key initiatives, at scale if possible, by keeping track of laws, regulations and major trends.

CHAPTER 2

ECOSYSTEMS AND ECOSYSTEM ARCHITECTS

Most megadeals involve dependencies on many organizations beyond the buying organization. We call this the megadeal ecosystem. It might include local, state or international authorities, related suppliers and distributors, interfacing systems, local communities, customers, consultants, etc. All of these entities could be affected by the changes that your offering will require. The megadeal ecosystem, in other words, is very different from that of normal complex selling. This chapter will help you understand the importance of the megadeals ecosystem and how to navigate it.

What is an ecosystem?

According to James Moore's definition, a business ecosystem is an economic community whose foundation is supported by a network of interacting organizations and individuals. He borrows the analogy from biological ecosystems and calls the participants in the business ecosystem "organisms." An organism in the business ecosystem could be a supplier, lead producer, competitor, or other stakeholder. "Over time," writes Moore, "they coevolve their capabilities and roles, and tend to align themselves with the directions set by one or more central companies. Those companies holding leadership roles may change over time, but the function of ecosystem leader is valued by the community because it enables members to move toward shared visions to align their investments, and to find mutually supportive roles."

He goes on to say that companies need to become proactive in developing mutually beneficial ("symbiotic") relationships with customers, suppliers, and even competitors.

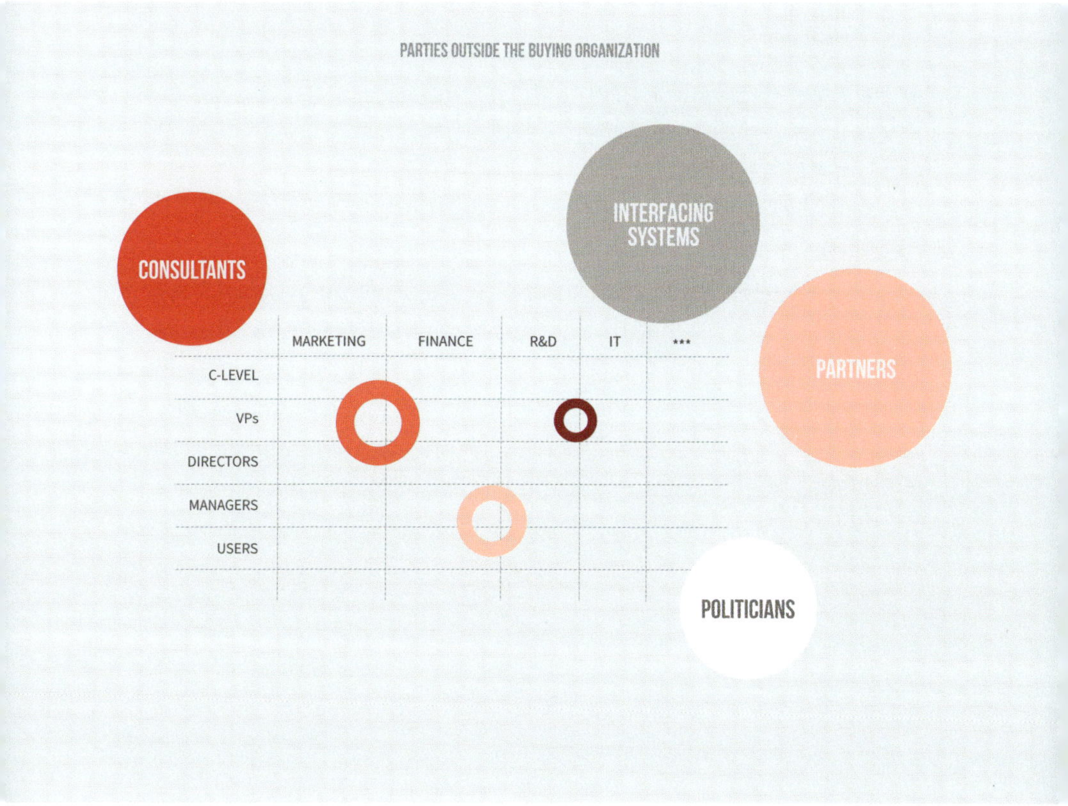

One of these ecosystems is not like the other

Low to medium complexity B2B selling involves 5-7 key stakeholders. This is why, in smaller B2B deals, if you have narrowed down the handful of stakeholders that you need, you're close to closing the deal. However, in a megadeal, you need to go far beyond a handful of people. A megadeal typically includes more than 100 stakeholders both inside the target organization and in the surrounding ecosystem.

This is why dialogue techniques (the main focus in most sales and marketing books), while still important, cannot be relied upon as the primary tool for closing a megadeal. Of course, you will still have one-on-one discussions, but you could never reach hundreds of stakeholders this way.

In basic B2B selling, there are four critical issues to cover:

1. The problem
2. The related solution
3. The business case (hard, soft or both)
4. The 5-7 key stakeholders in the buying organization

In contrast, a megadeal will require you to address the four points above within multiple functions and hierarchies. The illustration below shows an example where a selling party needs to win over stakeholders from a few different functions and levels of hierarchy. Map out which titles/ responsibilities you need to handle and list their names and contact details. (Note: Sometimes the matrix is a cube or an even more complicated structure.)

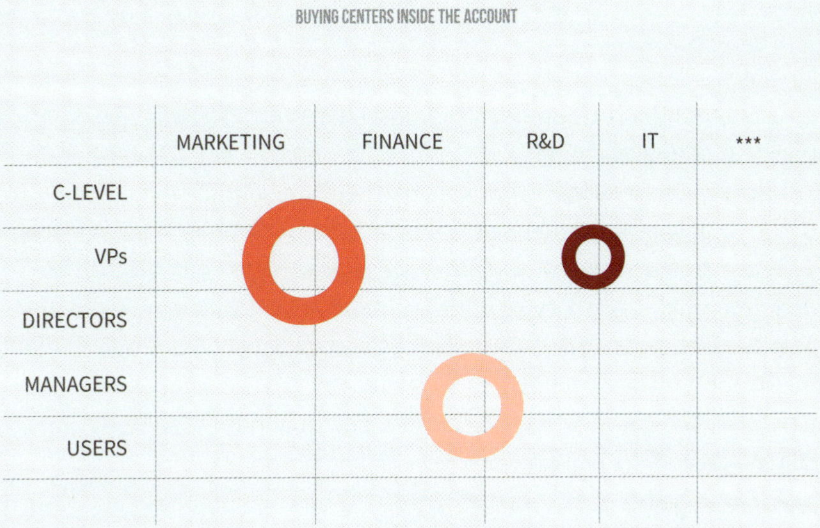

In a megadeal, you need to cover the points from basic and advanced B2B selling, and master a few additional aspects around the deal. You need to:

- *Understand the ecosystem* around the customer
- *Connect with stakeholders* inside the customer organization and inside the other organizations in the deal ecosystem
- *Add insight-based value* to the ecosystem
- *Shape the ecosystem* by becoming an ecosystem architect

Ecosystem mapping 101

Most megadeals are tech-based and have significant consequences. "The complexity and consequential nature of megadeals is why the decision journey is often so long," says Proof Analytics CEO Mark Stouse. "The ecosystem demands a lot of due diligence in order to bear against the damage that a bad decision might do to existing systems. Whether they involve building a bridge, an airplane, a software system, etc., you will have a set of related systems and related risks to those systems."

You need to understand which systems are affected, locate the boundaries between those systems, and figure out how your offering intersects with the surrounding ecosystem. This will also help you identify the most critical stakeholders.

But while the system approach will help you identify most of the parties involved, you still have to look at who has influence outside the system - in legal, finance, and other areas that might have a role in the decision-making process. As we mentioned above, a lot of megadeals involve politicians, various permitting authorities, or land owners, that might not be so easy to identify. This is where it helps to get the information directly from your main stakeholder or champion. Ask: What parties will the deal affect or involve? What local or national permits might you need? Who needs to say yes and to what? And what are those people's functions? Who needs to say yes on a financial level? Keep in mind that it might not always be the most obvious candidate.

It sounds simple, but read the news. Changes in large ecosystems have a ripple effect that will get noticed by the media and as a result reveal key stakeholders. We interviewed a few megadealers who approach each new deal like a CIA agent, obsessively looking at it from every angle, and reading every news story related to it.

In Chapter 4, we will discuss Trojan horses. They will also give you information that can help you identify key stakeholders in the ecosystem.

Finally, you will get most of the information you need to map the ecosystem from the key stakeholders themselves, simply by asking. If everyone understands the map, they can better help you, too. This leads directly to consensus, which we will cover in the next chapter, which is all about how to connect with and win over the ecosystem to your side.

A megadeal with a large organization is often cross-functional (finance/legal/IT), multinational and cross-hierarchy (involving everyone from the C-suite to the user level).

Planning

It is difficult to follow a strict plan when you are pursuing a megadeal. However, planning is often more valuable than the plan itself. Since megadeals often involve many parties internally and externally, including permits, etc., it will benefit you greatly if you can take the ecosystem and the matrix and see what needs to be done and in which order.

Many of the items on your list can be done in parallel, but a lot of them have serial dependencies. Create a timeline and plot the various parties, and things that need to fall in place, and then start to execute. It is often invaluable if you can be transparent about at least a version of your plan with the client. Ask them if they think it holds, and get them to at least shake hands on it. Most of the time this will make sense as the buyer knows that a megadeal sales journey is expensive for the vendor. A good buyer has no interest in wasting your time or resources since it will only affect your ability to deliver later on.

The negative stakeholders

It's worth mentioning that if the buyer's representatives are negative toward shaking hands on your plan, ask yourself and the account team whether the deal is worth moving forward with. This is a valuable qualifier. Again, megadeals are expensive to run, so a healthy dose of cynicism is required.

As megadealer Walt Parmer told us, "It's not just about finding the 'pro' stakeholders, you have to identify the 'cons' as well. Too many people are trying to identify the champions and the check-writers and not paying attention to who might have a vested interest in blocking the deal."

Another megadealer, Bora Brännström, told us about a deal he'd worked on for more than a year when he was at American Express. They had mapped out all the stakeholders in the ecosystem across every key function, from sales and marketing to procurement and compliance. There was only one person they hadn't approached.

"We had every cornerstone of a megadeal: we had alignment with a key initiative, we had mitigated their risk and we had everyone onboard - their CFO, CEO, and the rest of their management team, along with their marketing and sales team. We had multiple inside sources feeding us information. But even though we had asked several times if we should meet with the owner, we were told he was not operational and that the board decision was only a formality." Unfortunately, It turned out that the "non-operational" owner and two of his senior advisors were in fact pivotal decision makers, and the deal fell through.

Ecosystem architects

Experienced megadealers are like top goal-scorers in soccer - the players who score no matter which team you put them on. They have an ability to understand not only the ecosystem's current state, needs and drivers, but also what direction all of these are moving in. Being able to see macro-trends gives megadealers the information they need to position their offering and predict how each party will fit into the future state of the ecosystem. Megadealers who have this ability are what we call "ecosystem architects," because they have an innate ability to shape the ecosystem.

Konrad Bergström at Zound Industries is a good example. Back in 2009, most of us were using one headset for our phones and another for our iPods or music device. Bergström looked around, saw that all the cool kids had these fancy headphones, and decided to put a microphone on a pair of really cool headphones. Voila, the audiophile no longer had to use two sets of headphones. In effect, Bergström saw that the ecosystem was changing (that we would soon be listening to music on our phones) and that we would need a microphone on our hi-fi headphones in order to do so.

Konrad Bergström's next leap was to realize that the phone would soon replace the stereo system in our homes - which would require speakers kitted out with Bluetooth. But instead of developing speaker technology from the ground up, Bergström reached out to Marshall - the biggest name in rock concert amplification. Yet again, using his knowledge of the ecosystem, he knew that Marshall lacked the technology and the marketing knowledge to make this leap themselves. So he licensed the brand and launched a new line of Bluetooth speakers, kicking it off with a major event attended by Sweden's biggest snowboarding stars. Today, Zound is one of Sweden's fastest-growing companies, and the megadeal contract with Marshall has had a radical impact on Marshall's success, too.

Elon Musk is another famous example, both for making a desirable electric car, and for figuring out that all solar roofing panels needed in order to be appealing was to look like... roofs!

These ecosystem architects and shapers are common in the mega-deal world. They are also common among the greatest leaders. Ray Dalio (Author of *Principles*, which we strongly recommend reading) wanted to figure out if the most successful people in the business world had some common traits. Dalio asked a few of his friends and contacts, such as Jeff Bezos, Steve Jobs, Bill Gates, Elon Musk and a few others, to take a personality test.

These are the characteristics that Ray Dalio found to describe shapers that we also see in ecosystem architects:

- They are independent thinkers who let nothing and no one stand in the way of achieving their ambitious goals.
- They have strong visions of how things should be done, and a willingness to adapt and make improvements quickly with an open mind.
- They are resilient. Their need to achieve what they envision is stronger than the pain they experience as they struggle to achieve it.
- They have a wider range of vision than most people, either innately or because they have learned how to get insight from others who can see what they can't.
- They are able to see both the big picture and granular details (and the nuances in between).
- They are simultaneously creative, systematic and practical.
- They are passionate about what they are doing and want to have a significant beneficial impact on the world.
- In the personality assessments, all ranked low in the category 'Concern for Others'. When faced with a choice between achieving their goals or pleasing (or not disappointing) others, they would choose achieving their goals every time. Even Bill Gates, who devotes most of his wealth and energy to helping others, scored low.

In this chapter, we have focused on understanding the ecosystem. How to work with shaping the ecosystem to win megadeals is covered in more detail in the next chapter on consensus. Trust and risk mitigation are also pivotal in megadeals, and you will increase trust if you work with, and are accepted by, the whole ecosystem, not just by the buying organization or, worse, only the buyer and his/her closest staff. This will also be covered later in the book.

EXERCISES

Exercise #1

Run a workshop with a few representatives working with a certain type of deal in your most important segment.

- Brainstorm and agree on the matrix (see page 33) for a generic client in the selected segment.
- Brainstorm and agree on what types of information and parties should be a part of the ecosystem map (shown here).

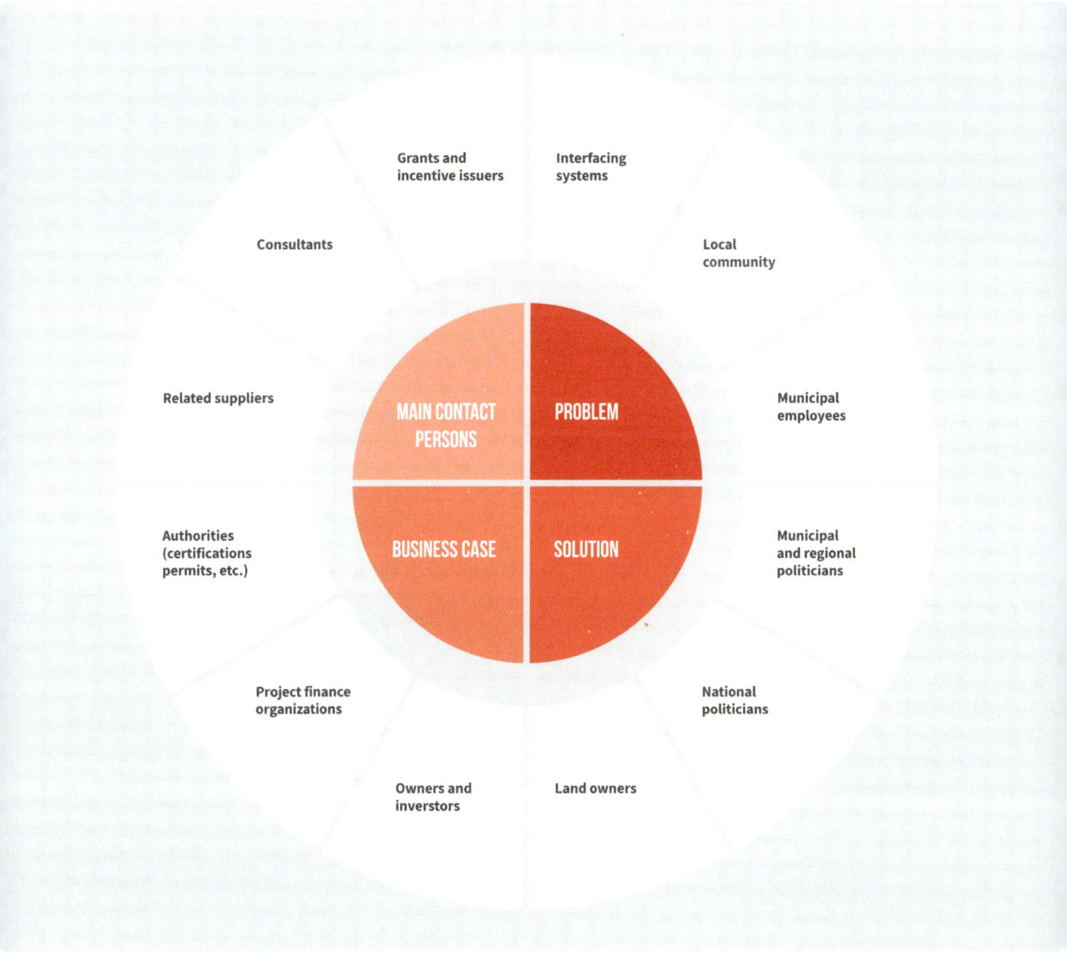

Exercise #2

- Use the results from above as an example and then repeat the exercise with representatives from each segment (we recommend doing this one-on-one).

Exercise #3

- Make the ecosystem and matrix per prioritized client. This will be based on the generic segment models created above, but now with real names and real data for each case.

Exercise #4

- Move the ecosystem and matrix mapping for each account/deal into a timeline. Once you have mapped an ecosystem for one type of case, you can use it as a template for other cases, as the type of stakeholders will be the same.

KEY TAKEAWAYS

1. A key difference between conventional B2B selling and megadeals is the number of stakeholders, not just in the buying organization, but in the whole ecosystem of organizations around a megadeal.
2. Understanding, connecting with, adding value to and shaping the ecosystem are what make winning a megadeal so challenging. Because of this, traditional sales training will not be enough.
3. Many megadealers are shapers, which is a trait common among many of the world's greatest leaders.

CHAPTER 3

CONSENSUS

Consensus is the Latin word for agreement, originating from the verb consentio, which literally means "feel together." It was first used in English in the 19th century by physiologists to describe when all parts of the body are acting together toward a given purpose. Just as a simple action like drinking from a glass of water requires several different parts of the brain, the skeleton, and many muscles all to work together, a megadeal will only be successful when the ecosystem is in consensus. Consensus is not only an outcome, it is also a group decision-making process. As a megadealer, your task is both to drive the decision-making process in consensus - and to arrive at consensus. As megadealer Walt

> **"VERY RARELY IS A MEGADEAL DONE BY ONE OR A SMALL GROUP OF PEOPLE."**

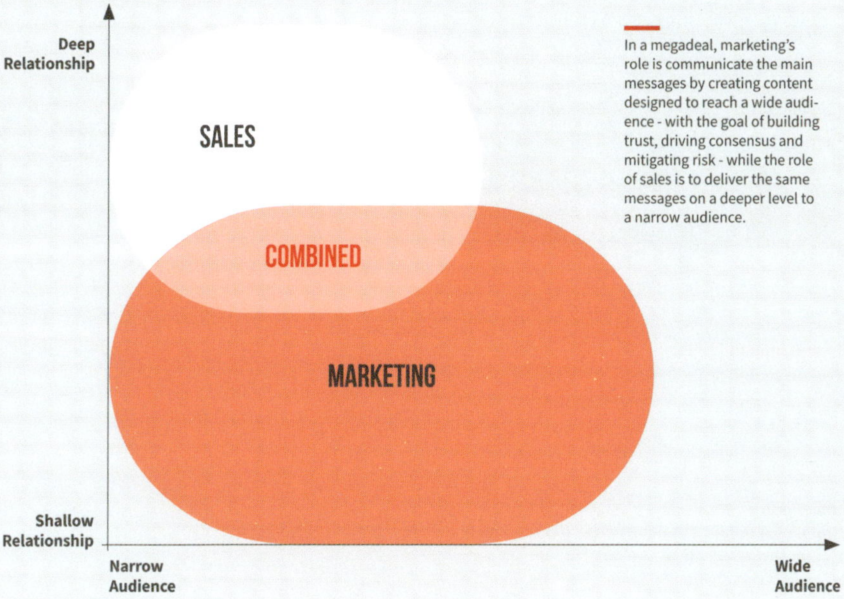

In a megadeal, marketing's role is communicate the main messages by creating content designed to reach a wide audience - with the goal of building trust, driving consensus and mitigating risk - while the role of sales is to deliver the same messages on a deeper level to a narrow audience.

Parmer told us, "Big deals are 30% technical and 70% political. Because of this, the key stakeholders have to take on your mission as their own. Only then will the deal get done."

Another megadealer, David Klättborg, recounted the experience of having sold a contract to a large global retailer when he was at American Express. The owner was so invested in the process that they set up a framework specifying which pieces of their internal ecosystem Klättborg and his team would need to engage - down to names and telephone numbers. There were two groups of stakeholders on the list that Klättborg admits he might never have considered otherwise: the cashiers and two people who entered transactions into the accounting system.

The cashiers turned out to be an easy sell - they were tired of having to turn AmEx cardholders away. But had David Klättborgs's team not reached out to those two people in accounting, they would have been in trouble - because guess who was seated at the table when the final decision was made? "With the pen literally suspended over the paper, the customer turned and asked those two individuals if they were comfortable adding our services to their system," Klättborg recalled. "It turned out all those meetings over coffee paid off!"

> **"IT TURNED OUT ALL THOSE MEETINGS OVER COFFEE PAID OFF!"**

Not everyone gets a map of the ecosystem from their potential buyer. Even if you do, how do you get multiple interest groups to agree to support your offering? Based on our interviews with the world's most successful megadealers, we have a few insights.

Challenges that make consensus creation important

As evidenced by the example above, megadeals often require that you sell both to the key stakeholders in the buying organization and to a mix of people in different functions and levels. Furthermore (and this is key), you will need to sell to the entire ecosystem of other organizations, government people, consultants, etc.

We mentioned in the last chapter that megadealers are often adept at understanding, connecting with, adding value to and shaping the deal-related ecosystem. They are also experts at interacting with various kinds of stakeholders, a skill that falls under dialogue techniques, which is covered in much of the sales literature. However, most dialogue techniques have been developed to help salespeople approach the C-suite. This can turn into a fatal flaw in megadeals, since it can lead you to overlook those two people in accounting or the vendor that provides your customer's IT. Those who excel at driving consensus know that they must interact with the ecosystem on every level. In Chapter 8 we'll share Johan Bjorklund's story of how he approached what was at that time the biggest deal in telecom history - by individually targeting almost 100 of the top stakeholders.

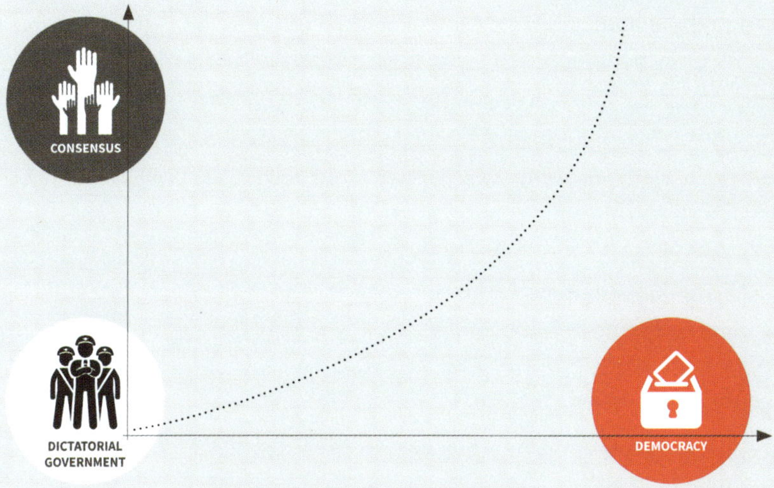

Consensus and geography

A quick note about geography and the need for consensus. Some cultures are more consensus-driven than others. Leaders in the democratic world need the support of the crowd before and after a decision, whereas countries with weak democracies tend to see more top-down decision-making. In Sweden, for example, heavy consensus creation is often required. The U.S. requires slightly less consensus, while Russia, India and Saudi Arabia have even less need for it. The latter three countries have a much more top-down approach.

However, because megadeals involve getting many organizations and related stakeholders onboard, consensus-creating techniques will be required even in the less democratic countries. Note that the above chart is not scientific but serves as an illustration to make a point.

Building large-scale consensus

A megadeal with a large organization is often cross-functional, multinational and cross-hierarchical, as described in the last chapter. If you cannot succeed in creating consensus at scale, you will run into problems making megadeals, since this is often required.

You may be tempted to pursue the process with the most engaged stakeholder. Or, another mistake, pursue the main stakeholder assuming that person is managing the internal selling process and the other stakeholders in the ecosystem. In both cases, you will realize only too late that by failing to create consensus in other critical parts of the ecosystem, you may have to start over - if you're lucky and have not lost the deal entirely.

Several meadealers in the U.S. told us stories of how they nearly lost the deal by failing to build consensus in their customers' IT departments - even though another area of the business was driving the deal internally on the client side. So even though the U.S. may be lower on the consensus scale, omitting a key part of the ecosystem could still place your deal in jeopardy.

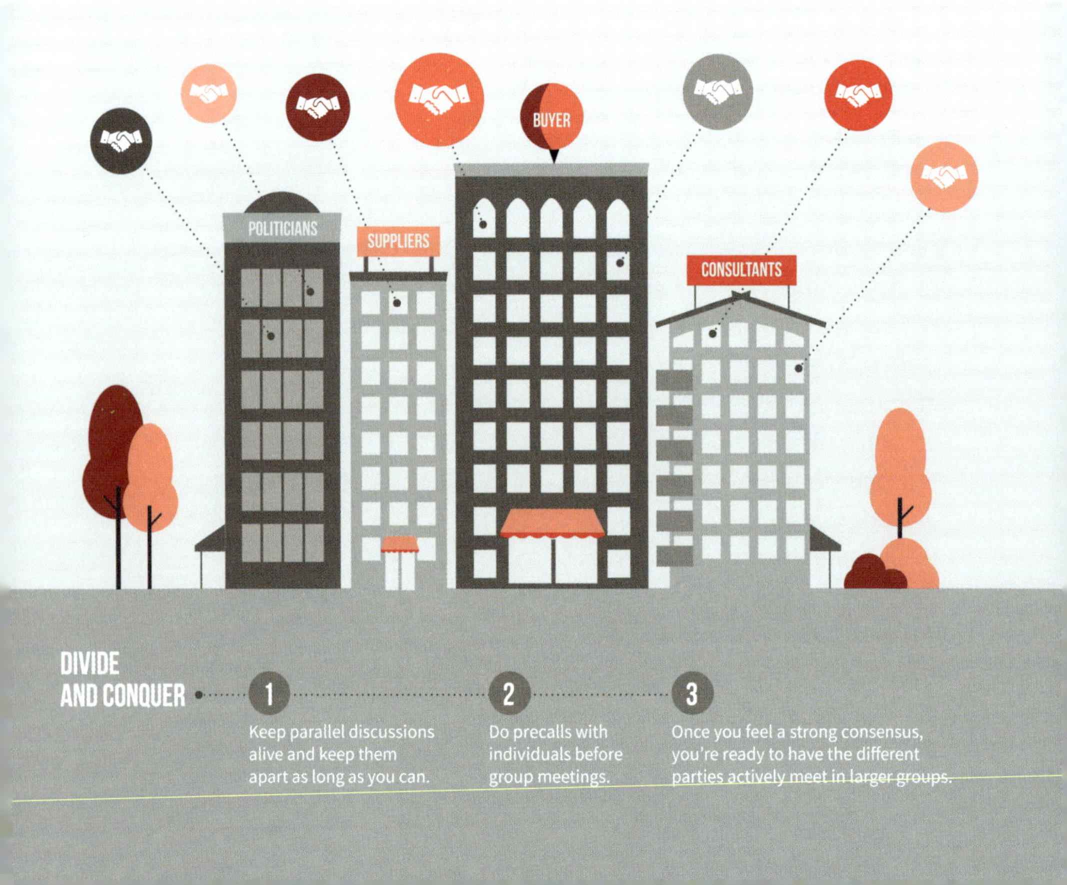

Because a megadeal creates major change in the buying organization, it often requires that you sell in the change, and that you sell it at scale (i.e., consensus-wide). When presenting a suggested change in a large organization, the person with the suggestion would never start with a microphone and address all the staff at once by asking if they think it is a good route forward. That would most likely lead to career suicide.

Mark Stouse often talks about how consensus is a function of three key decision psychographics: awareness, confidence and trust. "Awareness is exactly what it sounds like," says Stouse. "People have to understand their issues and questions as well as the concerns of their consensus partners before they can all begin to align. Confidence is all about competence: Do I believe that this will happen correctly and that it will add value, both for individuals and the group? Trust is defined as the absence of distrust. Do I believe that the others in the decision-making group have each other's best interests at heart? The answers to these questions impact the depth, quality and speed of consensus more than any other factors." We'll discuss the trust factor much more in Chapter 5.

If colleagues, suppliers, related politicians and all or many of the others in the deal ecosystem are talking positively about you and your account team, your company, and your solution, you stand a much higher chance of winning the deal. Group psychology is a strong factor. Overcoming consensus that has already been reached in another direction than yours is an uphill battle.

As mentioned above, we have seen in our research that megadealers are often really good at the following four things:

- *Understanding* the ecosystem (see Chapter 2)
- *Connecting* with the ecosystem
- *Adding insight-based value* to the ecosystem
- *Shaping* the deal-related ecosystem

We won't cover how to engage core stakeholders in this book. That is covered at length in traditional sales-related books on dialogue techniques. Instead, our focus is on how to handle the rest of the important-to-semi-important crowd inside the buying organization, along with the stakeholders in the rest of the deal-related ecosystem.

So how do you connect with the ecosystem?

As in any necessary interaction between people, you first need to establish a connection. You can be insightful and have a strong offering, but if you don't enter into dialogue with the various stakeholders inside the customer's organization and with other key stakeholders in the rest of the deal ecosystem, you will not succeed in creating consensus. Here we will mention a few ways to connect with large numbers of people so that you can get them interested, gain their approval, and align them behind your offer. We will review these in depth in Part Two.

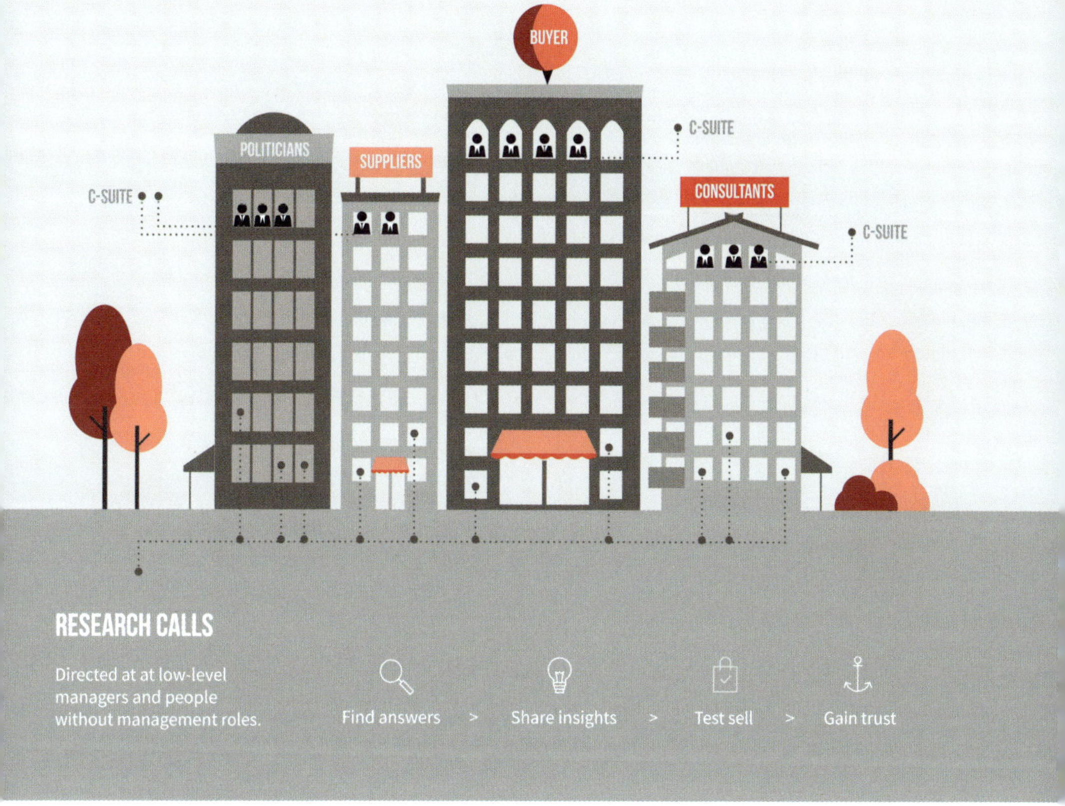

Research calls
While many of these stakeholders need to be on our side, and they need to be involved, they will not be the same individuals who sign the contract. The best method for reaching these people is through research calls. In a research call you have four goals:

1. Find answers to questions you have about key initiatives, the ecosystem, the most important individuals, and details related to your potential case with them.
2. Share insights about their industry (with this you gain trust and they open up more).
3. Test sell your offering and kindly ask for their suggested improvements (you want them to understand and like the elevator pitch).
4. Gain their trust and approval, and make sure it is OK for you to call back at some point. (This relates to the coming chapter about Trojan horses, and how you want to find people who are often lower down in the organization, who you can call to find out what is happening internally.)

BEE SWARMING

Directed at a vast number of stakeholders, including the key stakeholders. Bee swarming entails visiting the LinkedIn profiles of the stakeholders you want to later connect with on LinkedIn and eventually have calls/meetings with.

Bee swarming

In parallel with your research calls, and sometimes even beforehand, you should engage in what we call "bee swarming." Bee swarming entails visiting the LinkedIn profiles of the stakeholders you want to later connect with on LinkedIn and eventually have calls/meetings with. Most people look at who has visited their LinkedIn profiles and, with this tactic, you can drive their attention to who you are. Once they look back, you can gradually connect with more and more of the relevant people in your target account and in the ecosystem around the deal. (More in-depth information on social selling to follow in Chapter 8.)

Account-based marketing and account-based advertising

To further engage stakeholders in your target account and the other organizations in the deal-related ecosystem, account-based advertising is a good method for reaching a large audience in selected organizations. By using online advertising companies from the account-based

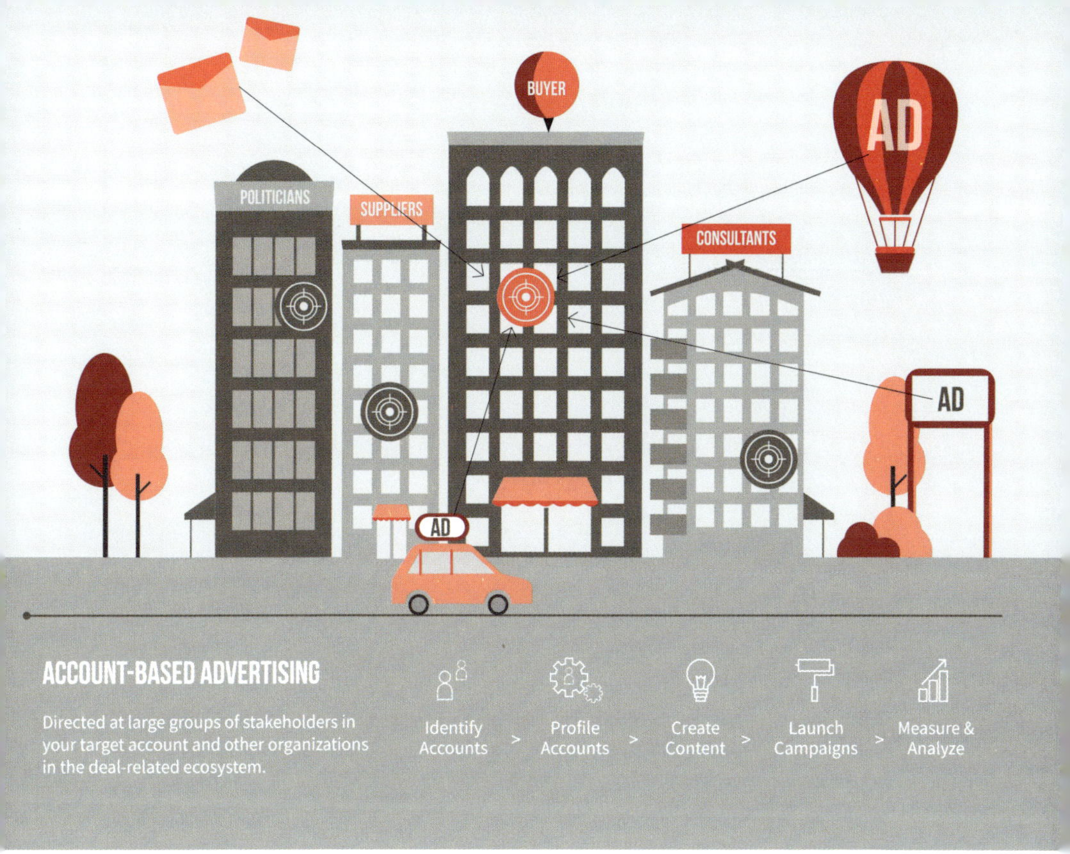

advertising category (such as Demandbase, InZynk, Jabmo, Terminus, Vendemore, etc.), you can show ads and videos via over 1,000,000 websites by targeting the IP addresses of the selected organizations. (Much more information to follow in the account-based marketing chapter.)

How to add insight-based value to the ecosystem

To gain and maintain access to a large group of stakeholders inside your target account and in the deal-related ecosystem, you need to give your audience insights. The first step to figuring out what insights they will find valuable is to look at the decision-making process from the buyer's perspective.

A buyer will move through four key phases in the decision-making process:

1. There is a problem I need to solve. Usually this problem is keeping them up at night - so much so that they will have put money aside to solve it.

2. What are the possible ways to solve the problem?
3. Why is one type of solution better than the others?
4. Based on how I've chosen to solve the problem, which vendor best meets my needs?

Thinking about the stages of the decision-making process from the customer's perspective will help you determine the fundamental messaging. The fundamental messaging serves as a guide to which insights to give your customer at each stage of the buying process. We will explain this in detail in Chapter 7.

How to shape the deal-related ecosystem

In Chapter 2, we discussed how to map the ecosystem, and we provided a few insights into ecosystem architects. Having the vision to see where the ecosystem is headed is an important skill; acting on that insight is a powerful tool when it comes to winning megadeals.

Doing so enables you to shift and frame the conversation, which in turn shapes the ecosystem. The film *Inception* offers a great analogy. Leonardo DiCaprio and his team are in the business of stealing people's ideas out of their subconscious minds. Then they get their toughest assignment - not to steal, but to plant an idea. To do this, they have to go even further down into their subject's subconscious so that he thinks the idea is his own. This is not unlike shaping the deal-related ecosystem. If you can plant the seed of an idea in the minds of the right people, the idea will grow until they begin to think of it as their own. Communicating industry trends and predictions is one way to plant the seeds for your idea across multiple channels.

This is what the cleantech company Climeon did during Christopher Engman's tenure. Digging wells is the most expensive part of a geothermal heat power project. It is often the biggest hurdle to success. However, the oil industry just happens to have numerous inactive pre-drilled well sites. In addition to existing non-productive wells, the oil industry uses, and wastes, vast amounts of hot water during the production of oil. It just so happens that a Climeon unit needs hot water to produce electricity.

Given that oil is peaking, and that the industry will likely soon be heavily taxed for its CO_2 emissions, Climeon decided to initiate discussion, and try to get people in the oil business to think about the next state of their industry. What if, without even deviating from their current core business activities, the oil and gas industry could transform into the best new bet in geothermal energy? In addition, oil companies often run off their own generators, or pay hefty fees to have cable laid down. More and more of them are actually not allowed to use oil for their own electricity production, so their operating costs are climbing. Sometimes their electricity bills are 60% of their total cost base. Having identified the change drivers and the industry's pain points, Climeon engaged top people in oil and gas on the issue, researched it thoroughly and wrote articles on the requirements for success. They even rented the Calgary Petroleum Club in Alberta, Canada, to run a breakfast seminar.

Along the way, Climeon managed to attract the interest of Breakthrough Energy Ventures, perhaps an even greater validation of the company's ability to shape the ecosystem. In the spring of 2019, Breakthrough, a green energy fund backed by investors such as Bill Gates, Jeff Bezos and Jack Ma, invested 12.5 MUSD in Baseload Capital, a project investment firm founded by Climeon to provide the capital to develop its power plants.

As the example above shows, if you can manage everything we've mentioned so far, and apply it using the tools and capabilities in Part Two of the book, you will be able to move easily between the levels of hierarchy and functional areas, generating all sorts of conversations in the ecosystem. Before you get started, however, we recommend that you identify your fundamental messaging as outlined in Chapter 6.

The fundamental messaging will help you know who to address on what level. Some people you meet will need to understand the problem you are attempting to solve and why it's important. They will understand the change driver - e.g., global warming and the transition from brown to green energy, putting old wells to work and taking advantage of waste water, oil companies need electricity onsite. Your stakeholders might understand the change driver but may not be convinced your category is the right one. In the case above, oil companies may see the need to supply electricity to their sites, but not understand why heat power is a better solution than fueling their own gas generators, or connecting to the grid with extra cables, etc.

Empowered with the map of the ecosystem, you will be ready to take on any journalist and deliver your messages as a public speaker inside and outside your industry. As in the Climeon example, once the company had mapped the ecosystem, and had their messaging in place, they were prepared to speak on the subject with everyone from engineers to drilling companies, operators, and politicians.

Internal consensus

When pursuing a megadeal, there is another angle on consensus related to your own organization. Almost all megadealers talk a lot about the need for internal consensus within their own companies. One megadealer told us that in one deal he managed at IBM, 499 people at the company had to sign NDAs because they were involved to various extents in a deal with a large African client.

A megadeal often involves a blend of your own products and services, which means it will involve multiple sub-organizations and even other vendors' offerings. So more than half of the selling you will do will be to your own organization, to align everyone internally and get them mobilized around the deal.

At Climeon, these deals required both internal lobbying and formal meetings where sales had to sell the case - in spite of the fact that Climeon basically has only one product. Each potential country and market segment had different pros and cons, and timing was key. Because the organization couldn't pursue every deal under consideration, there was naturally internal competition between cases.

We know of another company that even used IP-targeted ads to promote initiatives to its own staff. Because its people were located at different offices in different geographical locations, and some were even working out of their clients' offices, this tactic made a lot of sense. It is unwise to proceed with a megadeal without internal consensus, since every employee who is not onboard is a potential risk - especially if there are key stakeholders among them.

A few other learnings regarding how to create consensus

Divide and conquer is a strategy often used in politics, sociology, and economics in order to gain or maintain power, usually by causing disagreements among people who might otherwise join forces in a united front.

But what happens if you apply the "divide and conquer" tactic to the task of creating consensus as opposed to dissent? We have seen mega-dealers practice this with great success. By working separately to gain approval from different parts of the ecosystem, you will reduce the number of negative people. If you work with Net Promoter Scores (NPS), you will find this territory familiar. Simply apply the same metrics to your deal ecosystem - if you have people who are bad-mouthing you or your offering, that will have a negative affect on your positive references. In order to have a high win ratio, you will need to lower the risk of potential naysayers. Approaching people individually is one way to do this organically.

Here's what we recommend:

- Keep parallel discussions alive and keep them apart as long as you can. It is often unclear who is the real lead in an initiative. Don't encourage the client to get many people in the room at the same time. Even if it might seem advantageous to connect people who are not normally close to each other (from different countries, different departments, etc.), doing this too early on is likely to backfire.
- Before group meetings, do precalls with the individuals to make sure you have handled their potential objections before the meeting and have understood their objectives and perspectives. If you can align the individuals' goals with your own, you have a great advantage.
- Once you feel a strong consensus, you will benefit from actively uniting your parallel processes within the account and in the ecosystem. That's when you're ready to have the different parties actively meet in larger groups.

When we asked Walt Parmer how he knew when a client had taken on his mission as their own, he described a time when he was selling an AI platform to an oil and gas company. The operations executive was his champion and had spent considerable time with Parmer and his team to understand how the platform would help the company drill oil wells more efficiently.

However, the analytics team had already chosen a different platform and was reluctant to consider alternatives. "Our champion passionately canvassed for a reevaluation," Parmer recounted. "If we had attempted to overturn a prior decision from the vendor side, the deal would have died on the spot. Having one colleague talk to another was the only path forward." Parmer was able to progress his deal by understanding his prospect's prior investments and culture, and by having the champion help drive consensus in another part of the ecosystem.

Barriers to entry

An added benefit to creating consensus in the ecosystem is the long-term advantage of having created a tougher barrier to entry for any future competitors.

EXERCISES

- Workshop to list the questions you and the team can ask in research calls (and to which stakeholders).
- To enable ecosystem shaping, workshop to agree on the biggest trends affecting your client in your segment.
- To enable ecosystem shaping, workshop around what the future ecosystem could look like and why.

KEY TAKEAWAYS

- Consensus creation is probably the hardest part to master of everything we describe in this book. There are, unfortunately, no shortcuts.
- Consensus is critical in megadeals since there is almost always a broader ecosystem involved and not just one company's stakeholders.
- People tend to trust groups more than a single individual.
- Consensus is not only needed in the external deal-related ecosystem, but also within your own organization.

CHAPTER 4

TROJAN HORSES

Most of the time, megadeals are made with the largest companies and organizations in the world. As we discussed in Chapter 2, these organizations tend to be very complex. Because of the complexity of the deal-related ecosystem, it is crucial to gain information and intelligence at all stages of the deal-making process. If no one in the buying organization is feeding you information about what is REALLY going on behind the scenes, you are certain to lose the deal.

In one of our interviews, a megadealer we'll call Patrick told a story from early on in his career that involved the first system his company had ever sold to a public authority. Patrick had worked hard to develop a good relationship with Simon, a project manager on the customer side. "In the middle of the process, Simon took me aside and said that one of the consultants we were working with was not well-liked by his organization. The consultant had come from banking and was simply too corporate in his approach." Patrick had to ask himself if that was a change his team could afford to make. Then he replaced the consultant with a woman with a different background.

"Getting that information from Simon at that exact point in the sales cycle was crucial to winning the customer's trust," Patrick stated.

What is a Trojan horse?

You are probably familiar with the story from Greek mythology of how the Greeks, after a long siege, built a giant wooden horse that could hold a small battalion inside it. After the Greeks pretended to sail away, the Trojans brought the horse inside their walled city. During the night, the Greek soldiers climbed out of the horse and opened the city gates, enabling the rest of their forces to infiltrate Troy and win the war.

What is a Trojan horse in the context of a megadeal?

In a megdeal, a Trojan horse is the secret weapon that was there all along. You don't have to send one in like the Greeks - you just have to find the Trojan horses that already exist, hidden within the buying organization. If you don't have at least one Trojan horse in a megadeal, success is unlikely. However, there will be times, as in the case of public RFPs, when it may be virtually impossible to approach individuals within the buying organization, and those relationships will be extremely sensitive if you do.

- A Trojan horse is one or several people inside the buying organization that are "pro" you. They want you to win.
- They won't usually express their support for you openly, but can make a major difference behind the scenes.
- Trojan horses work as your GPS - the ongoing navigation that helps you understand what is going on. Where are you winning? Where are you losing?
- These individuals often share inside information with you because they believe that doing so is in the best interests of their organization.

TROJAN HORSES

	Trojan horses	Champion/sponsor	Power Sponsor	Mobilizer
Officially stands on your side	NO	YES	Probably, but doesn't have too.	YES
Decision maker	NO	NO	Not likely in a megadeal, but probably in a smaller deal.	NO
Does internal selling	NO	YES	Probably, but doesn't have to.	YES

A Trojan horse is NOT the same as a champion, a mobilizer, a sponsor or a fox

A Trojan horse should not be mistaken for a champion. A champion is typically a person of higher rank, or at least the power and influence to openly fight on your behalf. In order for somebody to be a champion, they need to have both influence (in order to persuade others to take action) and "authority" to either make the decision or to get someone with budgetary oversight to make the decision.

Champions need to be egg-breakers as well, ready to stick their necks out to back you when the going gets tough. A champion is like a sponsor within the client's organization who will sell on your behalf when you're not there. They will guide you through the decision-making process, introduce you to key players and decision makers, and alert you when things go wrong. In contrast to a champion, a Trojan horse is often found very near the application you are working on and is very often low in rank.

A Trojan horse is also not a fox, as popularly defined by Jim Holden, or the mobilizer of Challenger Sales. Holden's fox has power within the customer organization, "an individual at the center of influence" who "prewires decisions." Mobilizers, similarly, are "the go-getters, teachers and skeptics of an organization... individuals focused on driving productive change within their organizations." In contrast, a Trojan horse often does not have power, and often has little control over decisions or the ability to drive change. It could be a technician, a personal assistant, or a lower-level manager.

"I call them mushrooms," a megadealer named Sarah told us. "Because they grow in the dark. I always set out to find them because they often give you the right information at the right time to help you win the deal."

Sarah told us of a time when she was working on an RFP and a Trojan horse told her that his organization didn't operate on a normal calendar year, and that they were in fact close to the end of their fiscal year. "He didn't reveal huge secrets," Sarah explained. "That would have given us an unfair advantage. That one insight, however, was critical for understanding the organization's readiness to close the deal."

To be clear, champions are essential in order to close a megadeal, as are foxes. However, in normal enterprise sales, one champion is often enough. In a megadeal, you will need many champions, but you also need as many Trojan horses as you can find.

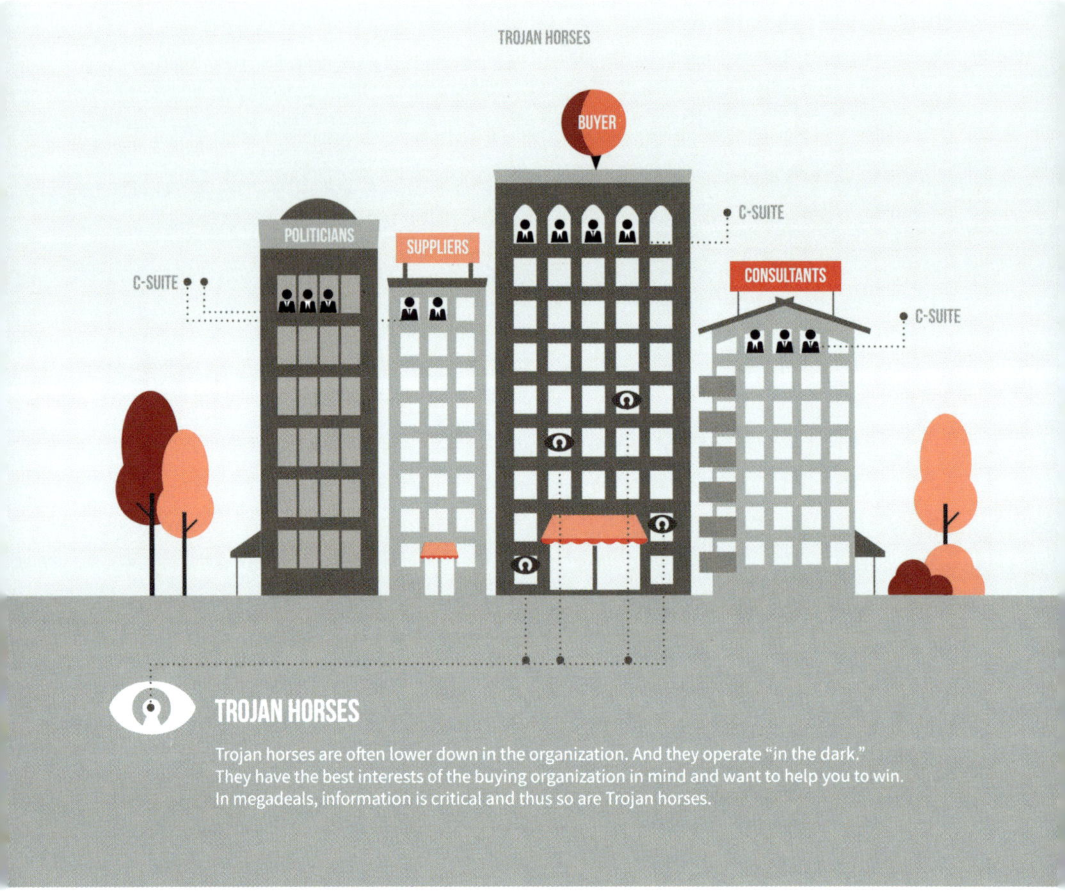

Trojan horses can help you answer the following:

1. What the key initiatives/strategic programs are (see Chapter 1)?
2. Who actually decides what - including which decision panels your proposal will need to pass, and what the decision criteria are in each committee or decision panel (if/when committees and decision panels are involved)?
    A. A title in an organizational chart is not the same thing as understanding who has major influence over a decision and who does not.
3. Who else is involved in the decision?

4. Who you are competing against?
    A. Who are the real competitors?
    B. Are you competing against the status quo? I.e., is the buying organization not doing anything, or have you landed in the low-priority trap? (See Chapter 1.) If your offer does not match up with a key initiative, then the status quo will be your toughest enemy.
    C. Are there substitutes (i.e., other categories of solutions that solve the problem in a different way)?
5. Who holds the budget for this project?
    A. Though this may seem obvious, the top decision makers are not always the same people whose budget the money will come from. Sometimes the funding for a megadeal is taken out of many budgets.
6. When a decision is likely to be made?
7. Who is for you, and who is against you, at all stages of the sales project?
    A. To have an open door with a few Trojan horses during the sales project might turn out to be your most valuable asset.
    B. You want many sources that can feed you with information on how things are going, leak information about competitive bids and competitors' strengths and weaknesses, etc., as well as information on who in the buying organization is pushing which vendor.

One important thing to note before you begin working with Trojan horses: you need to stay in touch with them, and this can be time-consuming. Like in any valued relationship, you can't just call them when you need them. You also need to give them insights if you want to get insights in return. It is not an exact trade, but you need to be valuable to them.

Because megadeals can take years to complete, you will likely need more than one Trojan horse - partly due to turnover, but also because different people will be able to help you at different points in the sales cycle.

How do you find the Trojan horses?

When making research calls (outlined in Chapter 3), you will come across people who tell you much more than you asked for and who express a strong will to change the area your offering addresses. A few of these individuals can be nurtured into Trojan horses.

During the sales process, you will also meet people who indicate that they have more to say. For example, you might find that one person in particular takes time to lead you out after a group meeting, and on the way mentions things for your benefit.

Like many of the megadealers we spoke with, Patrick, whose story we shared at the beginning of this chapter, confirmed that he has had at least one Trojan horse in every major deal. "I wouldn't say I have a strategy for finding them," he admitted. "But be a good listener. Try to really understand what they are saying. It's too easy to hear what you want to hear and not really what they mean. If you just listen, you will find them."

This probably doesn't need to be stated, but never call the Trojan a Trojan to their face. Identify them, nurture them, gather intelligence from them. If you do this well, these relationships will likely turn into lifelong friendships.

Assess your Trojan horses objectively

While having at least one Trojan horse is indispensable in a megadeal, it is not a guarantee that you will succeed. You may even have developed several and be counting on their input, but you must be able to assess them objectively. Can you trust them? Are their opinions and insights really valid? Which ones should you not use? It could even be that one of your Trojan horses is actually a double agent whose aim is to get information from you in order to feed the opposition.

In a megadeal, there will inevitably be people who approach you informally, but you always have to ask yourself if they might have another agenda. Of course, people will always have their own agenda: the trick is to make sure that your agenda is aligned with that of your Trojan horses.

HOW TO ASSESS YOUR TROJANS:

- Does this person have your best interests in mind as well as their company's or is this person a "double agent"?
- Is this person well informed?
- With the set of Trojans we have, will we get the right information?

In our interview with Mikael Philipsson, he told us about trusting one person as a Trojan too quickly. "We put a lot of trust in him because we thought he had more knowledge than he did. Because he really wasn't that informed, we didn't get the whole picture."

"A little paranoia is a good thing to have in these situations," Philipsson added. "I look for people with the same core values or a genuine personality - people who are transparent, trustworthy, and humble. Discussions with those types of people come naturally. You can just feel it. But still, I'm always quite cautious about choosing which ones to trust on the inside and which ones not to. That is always an internal discussion in my head and in these organizations because it could have the opposite effect."

In fact, in the megadeal Philipsson told us about, they almost lost the deal because a competitor actually had stronger Trojans. In the end, he was able to turn the situation around by mitigating the client's risk, which is the subject of our next chapter.

EXERCISE

Run a workshop to discuss how you can:

- Identify Trojan horses.
- Decide what information you want from them and when.
- Figure out how you can stay relevant over time with your Trojans.

KEY TAKEAWAYS

Since winning a megadeal requires engaging a whole ecosystem of stakeholders inside and outside the buying organization (as mentioned in Chapter 2), having a champion is not enough. You will need both many champions in megadeals, as well as many Trojan horses.

The differences between a champion and a Trojan horse are:

1. Champions have influence and authority while Trojan horses do not.
2. Trojan horses are, most of the time, much closer to the actual problem area you are trying to address (closer to the application).

If you don't have Trojan horses, you will probably not win a megadeal.

CHAPTER 5

RISK MITIGATION

Take a look at the examples below. In *Megadeals* seminars, we ask attendees to choose which solution is most likely to be selected in a megadeal context. The answer is not as obvious as you might think. While on a personal level you might be willing to invest in a cheap stock with a huge upside even if the risk is higher, large organizations are risk-averse.

There is a famous quote that goes, “You’ll never get fired for buying from IBM.” That’s because IBM is often considered the safe bet. Large organizations will almost always choose Alternative A since the risk is so much lower, even though the potential ROI is much less than with Alternative B and the price tag significantly higher.

This is important to know if you want to succeed in winning a megadeal. Too many salespeople spend too much energy on USPs and value propositions when actually risk is far more important to the customer. Not saying that USPs and value propositions are not valuable. They are. It is just pivotal to spend significant time and resources on mitigating risks, especially in the megadeals world. Furthermore, your customers will be willing to pay more if you can significantly reduce their risk.

ALT A	ALT B
100 MUSD	10 MUSD
1% RISK OF FAILURE	35% RISK OF FAILURE
13% ROI	189% ROI
112 MUSD (+12%)	18.8 MUSD (+87%)

What is risk mitigation or risk management?

Risk management involves identifying, evaluating, and prioritizing risks in order to minimize, monitor, and control those risks that might materialize as real problems. As illustrated in the example above, risk management plays a critical role in megadeals. By learning how to identify and mitigate your customer's risk, you increase your likelihood of winning a deal.

Why is risk important?

Because megadeals involve such large amounts of money and time, those who are involved in the decision-making process at both the selling and the buying companies often put their jobs on the line to make the deal happen.

Avoiding losing (or avoiding making a poor buying decision) is often more important than winning, especially when the stakes are high, like they are in megadeals. As Daniel Kahneman concluded in his Nobel Prize-winning research on loss aversion, we human beings have a 2.5 times stronger drive to avoid pain than to achieve pleasure. In light of this, sales and marketing people who are trained to talk about upsides, USPs and benefits are probably not taking into account how the brain really works.

If they did, they would see that they should be spending less energy on promoting the value and upside of a deal, and more on mitigating risks.

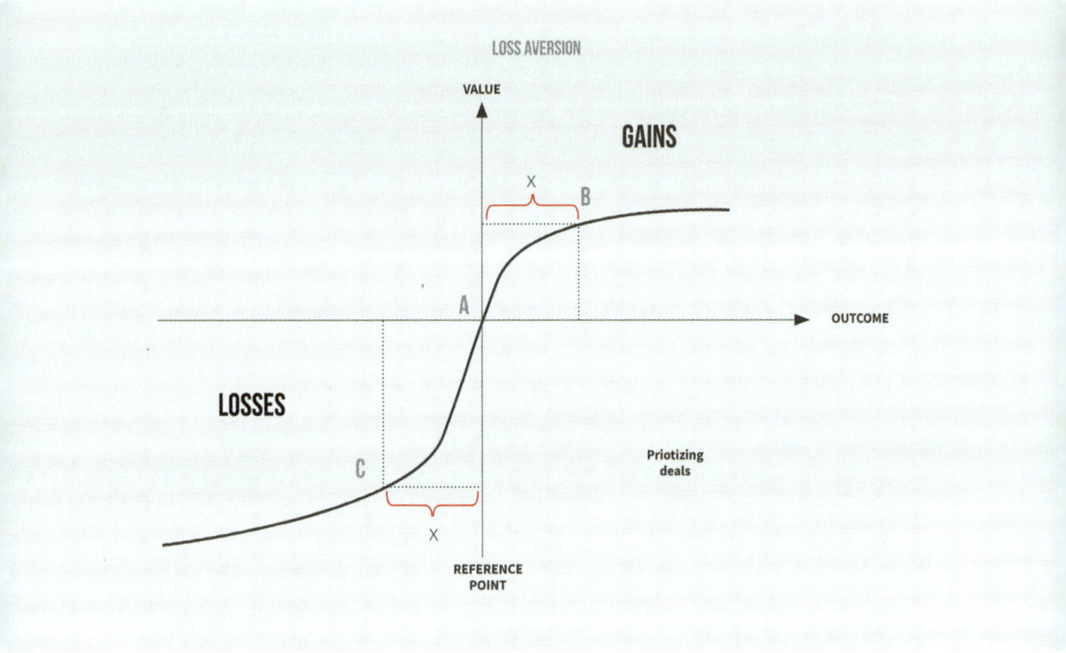

Johan Bjorklund, who orchestrated one of the largest deals in telecom history, recalled that it was roughly 18 months in the making - and that they were engaged in risk mitigation from day 1. “In deals like this, the client is giving such a large chunk of business to you that they want to make sure you have a sustainable business model,” he said. “In our case, they required full transparency around how we were making money. They wanted to see that what we were offering was actually at the core of our business.”

Risk is so important for buyers that it is usually more significant to improve the reliability of performance rather than achieve high performance. In most cases, buyers will use an interest rate, the Internal Rate of Return (IRR), that takes risk into account as well.

We often avoid talking about risk because it feels uncomfortable. If you don't speak about risks in the open with your client, you can guarantee they will speak about it without you present. That is a far worse scenario, since you won't hear what they say, won't know those risks exist, and won't be able to respond to the ones they have identified. By avoiding addressing potential risks and letting the client discover them on their own, you may also be seen as untrustworthy. It's worth noting that it is an emotional cost for the client to talk about the things they don't like about your offer, which is why they won't necessarily bring it up unless you push it.

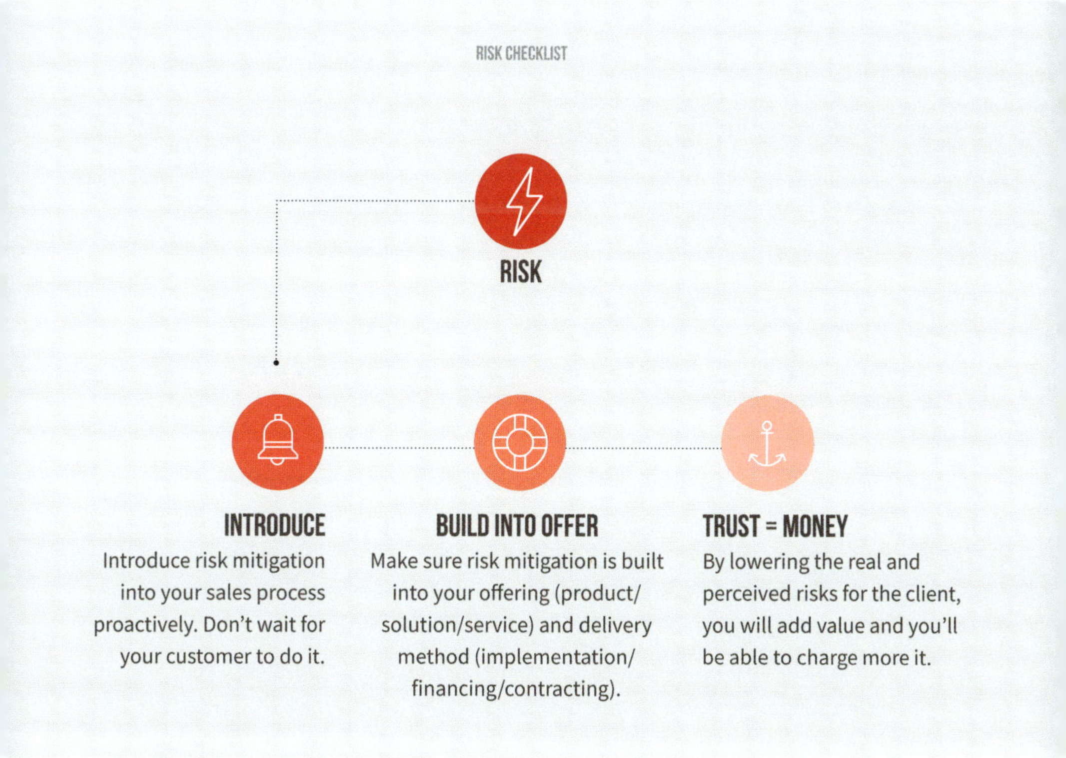

You can also split risk mitigation into four steps:

1. *Risk mitigation identification* is the process of identifying real and perceived risks first with your own colleagues and later with the cli-

ent. Many companies who are great at making megadeals have done very solid work around this.

2. *Risk mitigation planning* is the process of developing options and actions to enhance opportunities and reduce threats to the project's objectives.
3. *Risk mitigation implementation* is the process of executing risk mitigation actions.
4. *Risk mitigation progress monitoring* includes tracking identified risks, identifying new risks, and evaluating the effectiveness of the risk process throughout the sales project, implementation and on an ongoing basis thereafter.

It's important to develop a strategy that closely matches your company's profile, type of offering and target industry.

There are four main types of risk mitigation strategies:

1. *Risk Acceptance:* While it will not reduce the impact of the risks, risk acceptance is still a strategy. It is worth considering when the cost of taking on the risk is less than the cost of other risk management options (such as avoidance or limitation). One example is a company that does not want to spend a lot of money on avoiding risks that are unlikely to become a reality.
2. *Risk Avoidance:* This is the strategy of avoiding any exposure to risk whatsoever. The opposite of risk acceptance, it is usually the most expensive risk mitigation option.
3. *Risk Limitation:* This is the most common risk management strategy among businesses today. It limits a company's exposure by taking selected actions. This strategy employs risk acceptance and risk avoidance, and/or a balance of the two. As an example, take a steel plant that accepts failures in parts of the steel production process, but keeps very expensive spare parts on hand and a staff of service engineers on standby in case of major failures.
4. *Risk Transference:* This involves handing risk off to a third party. For example, many companies outsource operations such as customer

service and payroll. This can be beneficial if these non-core competencies represent a risk that another company is better suited to take on.

Real or perceived risks

Risks fall into two categories: real risks and perceived risks. Real risks might include the likelihood of a machine experiencing downtime x% in year 1, and y% in year 2, etc. A perceived risk might be that your brand is not accurately communicated, or that the client doesn't trust you personally. Which risks are real and which are perceived could be debated for hours, but these are the two types we will address.

What are some examples of risks?

Risks can come from almost anywhere: uncertainty in financial markets or currency fluctuations, the threat of project failure (at any phase of design, development, production, or long-term life-cycle), legal liabilities, credit risk, accidents, natural causes and disasters, deliberate attack from an adversary, intellectual property theft, or events of uncertain or unpredictable root cause.

There are real risks - like those related to performance, quality, price changes, bribery, etc. And then there are perceived risks - like a customer who worries that they might invest in your solution only to have a competitor release another generation of the same solution a year later.

Megadeals involve more risk mitigation than normal B2B selling both because of the complexities involved and the amount of money on the line. For this reason, we have included two chapters later on in the book that deal with risk mitigation when it comes to financing and drafting contracts for megadeals.

One of the most important risks that megadealers must work to address in the deal-making process is related to trust.

Lack of trust in the salesperson/sales team/solution/selling company

There are many ways in which the word "trust" can be broken down. For the purpose of pursuing megadeals, we find these four aspects especially fitting. Put yourself in the shoes of your potential buyer and ask yourself these questions to gauge their level of trust in you, your company and your offering:

Capability
Does this vendor and the allocated team have what it takes to deliver on their promises?

Vision
Does this vendor have a strong vision of the future?

When there is a strong and believable future vision, buyers feel that there is a higher chance that it's safe to stay with you in the long term.

A clear vision can also compensate for lower confidence/capability. Some people think that a vision is in contradiction with the truth. Yet many of the greatest companies and leaders in the world have powerful and credible visions of what the future will look like and how they will help their clients and themselves to arrive at that future scenario. This significantly mitigates both a perceived and a real risk. Who wants to tie themselves to a vendor that does not have a strong, clear view of the future? A vision also becomes more credible if you can accurately describe the history and the present - because it makes your audience more likely to believe in your description of the future.

Honesty
Can I trust that this company/team is telling the truth, and that when things don't go well they will solve it?

Consistency
Does the vendor/team have the capability and honesty to deliver the same results over a long period of time?

Examples of how you can mitigate trust-related risks
The points above about trust are the way we see it and packaged for megadeal sales and marketing. It will be addressed again in David

Frydlinger's chapter on contracts. As the megadeals of the future will probably be based more on relationships and incentive constructions than transactions, if trust in the relationship degrades, there is a high risk that the entire deal will fail.

Claudia Hammond, in her book, *Mind over Money*, quotes the historian Yuval Noah Harari, who says, "Money is the most universal and most efficient system of mutual trust ever devised."

"Money provides us with an abstract way of freezing trust," Hammond writes. "To stay safe and to prosper, we need to cooperate with each other. This is easy if you know someone well but cooperation with strangers requires a means of quantifying and exchanging that trust. This is what money can provide."

Is it any surprise, then, that mitigating trust-related risks is fundamental to winning a megadeal? The amount of money the customer is willing to part with is literally an expression of trust.

Author Stephen M. R. Covey (of *The 7 Habits of Highly Effective People*) also believes that trust is pivotal, though he breaks trust down a bit differently. He says two primary components of trust are related to character, while the other two are related to competency. Here we will take a look at Covey's four components of trust through the lens of megadeals to provide you with a second perspective.

Integrity (Character)

According to Stephen Covey, the first trust component is integrity. Most major trust violations are violations of integrity. In addition to honesty, Covey says integrity is made up of three other virtues.

- Congruency: Is your team acting in accordance with your company values, and are you following through on your promises? If one of your company's values is the environment, for example, but one of the companies in your supply chain is clearing Amazon rainforests, you have an integrity problem on your hands.
- Humility: Covey says, "A humble person is more concerned about what is right than about being right, about acting on good ideas than about having the ideas, about embracing new truth than de-

fending an outdated position, about building the team than exalting the self, about recognizing contribution than being recognized for it." It's not so surprising that many successful megadealers often go so far as to point out the benefits of going with the competition, and are even willing to point out the risks of choosing their solution. Of course, these are also confident individuals who believe their solution is better or they wouldn't be pursuing the deal - but you get the point: if the potential buyer sees you as arrogant and lacking in humility, you will not gain their trust nor win the deal.

- Courage: Eleanor Roosevelt said that courage is when, "you must do the thing which you think you cannot do." Are you prepared to do what you know is right, regardless of the consequences? This could mean walking away from a deal you've worked on for some time - or, as in the case of Mikael Philipsson, not accepting rejection. Philipsson shared a story with us about a deal that fell through after he'd worked on it for years. The buyer had selected a competitor. Philipsson tried to approach the key decision-maker to find out what had happened, but to no avail. However, he was so certain that his solution was better for the client that he left a voicemail early in the morning saying he was flying over to London and hoped they could discuss it in person. Of course, decency prevented them from letting him sit on the stoop, so they met with him, and in the end Philipsson's company won the deal. But how many people would have had that kind of courage not to accept the rejection? If you want to be a successful megadealer, courage is a prerequisite.

Intent (Character)

The second component of trust is intent. Like integrity, intent comes from an individual's character. It is part of our value system. It is how we know we should act. Stephen Covey breaks intent down into three parts.

- Motive: Why do you do what you do? Is it clear to your potential customers? Covey says the best motive in building trust is to genuinely care about people. Do you care about your customer and their customers? One megadealer named Ellyn, who had worked at Microsoft,

Oracle and Dupont, told us, "You have to think: How can I help the person sitting across from me achieve more, so that he wants to do this job, and is so good with his budget that he can be promoted?" For her, the deal was never the end game. "Listen, no one is confused about the fact that you are trying to sell them something," she told us. "But remember: the technology, or whatever you're selling, is really just a means to an end - and the end is much more important to understand."

- Agenda: Your agenda is a result of your motive. What is your agenda? Is it obvious to the client? Are you being completely transparent? And if something is holding you back from being transparent, you'd better examine that closely - it could be an indication of a fault line that will rupture into a much deeper chasm later on in the deal or the contract.
- Behavior is how you follow through on your agenda. Behavior is important because it is what people see and judge. Does what you do and how you behave represent your agenda and stem from your motives? Case in point: Not only did Ellyn say she wanted her clients to succeed, she bought stock in every one of their companies and attended their shareholder meetings. Many different behaviors serve to increase trust, from simple things like being on time and saying what you mean to disclosing risks to the client before they figure them out themselves.

Capabilities (Competency)

Stephen Covey's third component of trust has to do with capabilities. We have addressed this briefly above, but we think every megadealer would benefit from examining capabilities through Covey's lens. He uses the acronym TASKS: Talents, Attitude, Skills, Knowledge, and Style.

We suggest examining each of these on a corporate level and individually. Do you and your company have the talent required to deliver? How about the attitude? The skills? If there are gaps in your knowledge, how will you fill them? Style has to do with your unique way of doing things. Companies, like individuals, have style - often expressed in terms of brand attributes or personality. All of these are worth reviewing in terms of their potential to validate and solidify the level of trust in the relationship. They are also worth evaluating as to the risk they represent if the actual level of competency does not match the customer's expectations.

If you need to build up your capabilities, focus on the strengths of your company and your offer. Remain relevant by continually increasing your knowledge and improving your skills, and stick to your vision as mentioned above.

Results (Competency)

Stephen Covey's fourth trust component has to do with results. We believe this is strongly connected to behavior (mentioned above). If your motives are true, and your agenda is clear, results should be the natural consequence of your actions. Most importantly when it comes to mega-deals, no one trust people who don't deliver results. Results are what you contribute to your company and your customers. Covey states, "... if the results aren't there, neither is the credibility. Neither is the trust. It's just that simple; it's just that harsh."

Potential clients will evaluate your past results and current behavior in order to assess your credibility and set expectations of what you will accomplish in the future.

Stephen Covey says if you want to improve your results, take responsibility for them (not just for activities performed). Second, he says, expect to achieve your goals. "Expectation becomes a self-fulfilling prophecy," said Robert Rosenthal, professor of psychology at the University of California, Riverside. "When teachers have been led to expect better intellectual performance from their students, they tend to get it. When coaches are led to expect better athletic performance from their athletes, they tend to get it." Finally, Covey says, finish strong.

EXERCISE

Hold a workshop to:

- Brainstorm all of the possible risks that a customer takes on when buying from you, including which ones are real and which are perceived.
- Discuss the severity of each (both the probability of occurrence and the consequences/cost if the risk becomes a reality).
- Discuss how each can be mitigated.
- Start to use this in customer meetings, marketing material, etc. (Again, low risk is more important in closing a megadeal than an aggressive IRR.)
- Perform a trust assessment from your customer's perspective.

KEY TAKEAWAYS

In megadeals, risk mitigation is more important than simply offering the client high returns - and in fact, it will more likely involve the promise of steady returns. Risk mitigation adds trust and increases the chances of mitigating those risks if you bring them up with the client before they do.

PART II

TOOLS AND CAPABILITIES

PART II

TOOLS AND CAPABILITIES

Let's repeat the five cornerstones in the *Megadeals* framework:

1. Key initiatives: Identify key initiatives and make sure your offer fits one or many of them. This should be the first step - and the easiest.
2. Ecosystem: Understand the deal-related ecosystem since these decisions involve many internal stakeholders (often 100+) as well as individuals and organizations outside the buying organization. We have seen cases where the vast majority of the stakeholders have remained unknown to the vendor throughout the buying process.
3. Consensus: Drive consensus in the ecosystem. You need to win "votes" in order to be prioritized, maintain momentum and, finally, win the deal. Since there is a vast and often unknown number of stakeholders in the deal-related ecosystem, it is time-consuming and often impossible to engage in dialogue with all of them - unless you use media and social media in a megadeal-specific way.
4. Trojan horses: Find and work with Trojan horses. To build a substantial amount of intelligence around a megadeal, you need to have a

few informants. These individuals are often far down in the organization but they can provide valuable insights. However, reaching them, and reaching many of them, can be challenging. You can't know in advance who they are.

5. Risk mitigation: To win megadeals, you need to focus more on risk mitigation than on describing value and differentiation. Not because value and differentiation aren't important, but because risk mitigation is more important. Risk mitigation includes mitigating both real risks and perceived risks. Communicating risk mitigation to a large audience is a challenge. It is not easy to get a vast number of stakeholders to see both the megadeal and the vendor as less risky.

In the next four chapters, we present what we believe are the most important tools and capabilities for nailing the cornerstones above.

1. Dialogue techniques: The first thing you will need to succeed in a megadeal is a foundation in B2B sales training. For the less experienced, this chapter will serve as a fast track to get you up to speed. If you are quite senior in sales, it will be more like a refresher course, but you will still gain insights into the gaps in traditional dialogue techniques, where they will not be enough to compete on the megadeal level. In the next chapter, we provide snapshots of established dialogue techniques such as Solution selling, Challenger Sale, SPIN, etc.
2. Messaging architecture: When pursuing a megadeal, it's critical that sales and marketing synchronize the messaging to megadeal customers. Our messaging architecture is designed to ensure that your sales and marketing team is on the same page as you target your customers throughout the various stages of the decision-making process. The messaging architecture should be seen as a key companion to your company's brand book, and a reference for all your marketing and communication.

CHAPTER 6

DIALOGUE TECHNIQUES

At least 80% of traditional selling is about how to engage in dialogue with your stakeholders. If you are not familiar with these techniques, we have provided an overview here - but we recommend that you read one or more of the great books that have been written on the subject. See the list below. These "dialogue techniques," as we call them, will provide you with an important foundation for deals of any size. Without them, you will definitely be out of your depth in a megadeal or in any B2B deal for that matter. In this book, we assume that you already know and use one or a mix of dialogue techniques.

Using dialogue techniques in a megadeal

Most dialogue techniques are designed for deals where there are very few people on the customer side. There are some dialogue techniques that are specifically designed for complex B2B selling that can also be applied to both traditional B2B sales and megadeals. In this book we will not cover how dialogues are run in a smart sales process. Nor is it our objective to disqualify those or to use new words for the same things.

However, it became clear during our interviews that because there is no literature or other training on megadeals, the question of how to use traditional dialogue techniques in a megadeals context has not been addressed. Furthermore, what we have found is that the education on traditional dialogue techniques tends to be too narrow for aspiring and even experienced megadealers.

If you are a seasoned salesperson or megadealer, this chapter will be repetitive for you. But practice makes perfect. We are true believers in the value of mastery. A quick review of these dialogue techniques together with our megadeal framework will better prepare you for operational excellence.

Recommended sales literature

There is a lot of great sales training out there, and many books on dialogue techniques that compete for the attention of B2B sales reps and managers. During our careers, we have studied the following, and we recommend reading at least one or two:

1. *The Challenger Sale*
2. *Customer-centric selling*
3. *Insight selling*
4. *The Sandler Selling System*
5. *SNAP selling*
6. *Solution selling*
7. *SPIN selling*

In this chapter, we will cover what our research has indicated are the most important aspects of these dialogue techniques when you are pursuing a megadeal.

The main components of dialogue techniques often include some variation of these five:

1. Analyzing, discovering and growing needs
2. Connecting and building trust with different personality types
3. Challenging and shifting beliefs
4. Finding or creating compelling events
5. Identifying and developing champions, sponsors and/or mobilizers

1. Analyzing, discovering and growing needs

If there is no need for what you are selling, no one will buy it. It couldn't be more basic. That's why the first cornerstone of a megadeal is nailing Chapter 1, Key Initiatives. You must first align your offering with your buyer's strategic programs, i.e., the expressed needs of the organization.

These needs come from either the desire to gain something or to avoid losing something (i.e., moving towards pleasure or away from pain). More specifically:

- Moving away from a problem that you have today
- Moving away from a problem that you risk having in the future
- Avoiding missing an opportunity that you have
- Moving towards an opportunity that you have

As David Sandler has often been quoted, "People make buying decisions emotionally and justify them logically." The human ability to use logic and our ability to connect with other people are among the things that separate us from animals. Our large and complicated forebrains are distinct from those of other vertebrates. But only part of our brains (the prefrontal cortex) deals with complex cognitive behavior. The oldest parts of our brains (the reptilian brain and the limbic system) are responsible for emotion. As you may know, the amygdala in particular is responsible for behaviors encoded in us for thousands of years, and this causes us to make decisions based not on logic but on emotion - in particular fear. When you are building up the need for what you are selling, it is absolutely essential to appeal to both the logical and emotional parts of the brain.

Let's look at three examples. As you will notice, the logical and the emotional drivers can either pull in the same direction or different directions - and they can be used to out-position your competitors. However, a word of caution on how you build on and appeal to the emotional pains/pleasures of your stakeholders: certain issues might be culturally unacceptable or offend people if addressed incorrectly.

LOGICAL	EMOTIONAL
Realizing a gain of 89 MUSD in ROI by relocating the factory.	Fear the management losing credibility in the eyes of investors and the public if you can't achieve your targets
Newly developed buying journey will raise NPS score from 50 to above 65.	Desire for the validation of a global marketing award for the marketing team
Buying from the market leader, despite lower performance and higher price tag	Fear of being fired for buying from a lesser-known vendor that might be unable to deliver if they encounter financial trouble

Analyzing and discovering needs requires research, which can be carried out in several different ways. We advocated for this in both Chapter 1 on Key Initiatives and Chapter 3 on Consensus, with the research call methodology. We also want to address the fact that many sales books talk about how to use questions. Questions are an extremely important tactical tool. To cover the topic here would take too much space. It is worth noting, however, that one of the key insights that differentiates *The Challenger Sale* from other sales methodologies is its approach to important key stakeholders. As Matthew Dixon and Brent Adamson stated in their book, executives no longer tolerate situation and problem-oriented questions such as, "What keeps you up at night?" You should know the answers to these sorts of questions long before you enter meetings at that level - and you will if you have read the first part of this book. And in the next chapter, Messaging Architecture, we will give you a framework to differentiate and tailor your messages in order to grow the need for your offering.

2. Connecting and building trust with different personality types
People are wired differently. Some people are more focused on results while others are more focused on other people. Some are more focused on the big picture, and some are more focused on the details. Some are more focused on winning while others are more focused on not losing. Of course, people have more differences than depicted by this description. What is important is that megadealers must be able to build trust and connect with people of all personality types.

We discussed trust in detail in Chapter 5. If you recall, we find these aspects to be the most important in a megadeal:

- *Capability*
- *Vision*
- *Honesty*
- *Consistency*

We also want to mention how important it is to be outstanding in personal communications where winning trust is concerned. A skilled megadealer should be good at:

- Creating rapport, i.e. connecting with people on a subconscious level. Matching, pacing, and leading.
- Personal storytelling has been used since humans could scrawl on rocks, and is still equally effective because of how our brains work. Using storytelling in the right way lets us communicate with the subconscious part of people's brains.

- Outstanding written communication is a skill that has become even more important over the years, especially now with social media and different devices that allow people to communicate in far more ways than even ten years ago.
- Outstanding workshop and presentation skills are core competencies because many of the interactions will take place in a meeting format. Standing out in this setting will also make you a candidate for speaking at industry events and conferences.

Trust is a part of every methodology - building trust and managing risk, the enemy of trust. The more money on the table and the higher the risk, the more you must build trust and mitigate the risk. In a megadeal, while there is no doubt that you should know the basics of building trust with different personality types, you must also be able to build trust in the category, subcategory, vendor and team/individuals, as we'll discuss in the next chapter.

When you are selling something simple, no one will expect you to know the other categories, or even all of the viable options in the subcategories. If you are buying a fan to use out in your garage, you might not care if it breaks down in a year, but if you are buying a Heating Ventilation Air Conditioning (HVAC) system, it's too big an investment not to do your homework. Megadeals are like this but on an even larger scale. Knowing the competitive landscape, USPs, and values is essential in a megadeal, but they are basic. Because the risk is so much greater, real or perceived failure cannot be an option.

In traditional B2B sales, you might be building trust among 3-5 people. Megadeals require that you build consensus among sometimes hundreds of people, and that forces you to sell and market yourself in a different way. It's not unlike running a political campaign. In fact, we recommend megadealers closely watch winning campaigns and the people behind them.

We spoke with Alice Heiman, a leading expert on complex selling, who runs a sales strategy firm in the U.S. focused on building world-class sales organizations in high-growth B2B companies. "An experienced megadealer knows how to talk to each individual that has influence on the buying organization," she told us. "They know how to find and use insights that are productive in group conversations because they understand where each person is coming from. They use what they learn to ask good questions that make people think and talk with each other and bring them to consensus by showing them where they agree and disagree. They become a facilitator. They understand they need to mitigate the client's risk and show the reward before closing the deal. If you are good at this, you will win more deals because what the customer sees is someone who has their best interests in mind."

3. Challenging and shifting beliefs

The authors of *The Challenger Sale* address the question of challenging and shifting beliefs in a great way with their concept, "teach, tailor and take control over the sale." In our experience, the best salespeople have a strong ability to challenge their clients in a way that does not offend or threaten them because they:

1. Have a deep understanding of the ecosystem surrounding each client's business so that they understand the past, the present, and the future in terms of threats and opportunities. This enables them to identify what keeps their clients up at night or, even better, what should be keeping them up at night.
2. Have the courage to point out the elephant in the room and actually speak the truth even when it is uncomfortable to do so.
3. Have the ability to orchestrate multiple customer dialogues during the buying journey and are able to shift the beliefs of large groups of people. In a megadeal setting, this is of extreme importance since there will likely be more than one hundred people in the extended target group. We'll give you our approach for how to go about this in the following chapters.

4. Finding or creating compelling events

In typical and complex B2B sales, a compelling event is often used as the reason, or reasons, why the client should buy *now*. They can be real, or manufactured by the sales team. Without a compelling event connected to your offering, it can be difficult to win a deal.

Compelling events can be global, regional, industrial or only affect one company. Changes in laws or regulations can be strong triggers.

Here are some other examples:

1. New legislation
2. Ending fiscal year
3. Increased prices
4. Current issue the client has that needs to be solved by a certain date
5. Delays in a project as a consequence if x is delayed
6. Seasonal factors such as Christmas shopping
7. Fulfilling a promise that was made to a boss or to the markets by a certain date

Compelling events can, of course, also be emotional consequences of something that happened that should not have, or something that has not happened that should have. An example of that is the loss of respect in front of shareholders, bosses, colleagues, or even family. More serious consequences might be getting fired or demoted. In our experience and research, logical reasons are commonly used as motivation to colleagues but emotional reasons are the real reasons.

In a megadeal, compelling events are less important as a sales tool per se. It is highly unlikely that you will be able to use a compelling event as leverage to make the decision happen faster. For instance, you cannot convince the buying organization to buy before the end of the month when you plan to change your price list. A compelling event for a megadeal might be a milestone, or a pilot project. However, even when faced with industry-wide penalties for non-compliance, there is no guarantee that the deal will happen faster, because a megadeal must still move through the various stages of the internal buying process.

As we mentioned in the last chapter, the kinds of large organizations that engage in megadeals often have a strong defense, i.e., there is a stronger drive to avoid losing than there is to win. Megadeals often require massive transformation, and therefore entail a lot of risk. Risk mitigation work is essential because of the magnitude of change and complexity involved - both for the buyer and the seller. In almost all cases, a megadeal has to be cleared by multiple buying committees all the way up to the board.

So while a compelling event might be the reason for the change, as we will discuss in the next chapter - not all compelling events can serve as change drivers behind a megadeal. In fact, in a megadeal, there is sometimes no compelling event, but rather an ongoing major pain, with no time or date attached.

A compelling event might be the reason behind a key initiative (as detailed in Chapter 1), but you do not need a key initiative in regular B2B sales. You do need to identify the pain and the relevant solution, find the relevant handful of decision makers and make a business case. These are, perhaps obviously, fundamental in any deal. But in a megadeal, as we discussed in Chapter 1, identifying a key initiative will help you ensure that there is a large enough budget, authority, an expressed need and a timeline to match your offering.

5. Indentifying and developing champions, sponsors and/or mobilizers
Different sales methodologies use different ways of describing the various people inside the buying organization who, each in their different way, support the selling organization. In Chapter 4, we described the importance of having a Trojan horse. Here are a few other types of people discussed in traditional B2B sales literature who will also be helpful in a megadeal.

Sponsor/champion
A sponsor or a champion is the person who helps you with internal selling, supplies information, and helps you get access to decision makers or a "Power Sponsor," as the role is called in the Solution Selling methodology.

Power Sponsor
Part of the Solution Selling methodology, the Power Sponsor is a person

so high up in the organization that he or she "can get it if they want it." This might be true in traditional B2B-selling, but it is rarely true in a megadeal. In many megadeals, even the CEO cannot make the decision by her/himself.

That said, the Power Sponsor can guide you anywhere you want to go in the buying organization, as well as show you how the organization works. This person could also be your main source for mapping the eco-system, and (intentionally or not) introduce you to Trojan horses.

Mobilizer

In the book *The Challenger Customer*, the authors differentiate sponsors from mobilizers. The mobilizers are the people who will help build consensus by "rallying the troops." *The Challenger Customer* also puts mobilizers into different personality types: the Go-Getter, the Teacher, the Skeptic, etc. (there are seven in total).

Summary

One of the reasons we decided to write this book is because we noticed a gap in the traditional sales literature when it comes to managing deals of this size and complexity. But we are big fans of the existing literature. You need to master one or a mix of the dialogue techniques to be able to win megadeals. Each approach adds something different to the discussion, and each has different nuances and applications. If this was all new to you, we recommend that you back up and read them all as soon as you finish our book.

EXERCISE

Take a minute to reflect on the five cornerstones we've laid out this book, and how they fit into your current toolbox of sales techniques.

1. How can you apply traditional sales techniques to your megadeal? On the flipside, are there any potential pitfalls, where you might rely too heavily on certain techniques that will not serve you well in a large and ultra-complex deal?
2. How can you draw on your knowledge of dialogue techniques to navigate, shape and build consensus in the ecosystem?
3. Consider your approach to identifying Trojan horses, champions and sponsors and the different types of information and help you will need from each type of person along the way.

KEY TAKEAWAYS

1. You should know how to analyze, develop and grow your customers' needs. In normal B2B sales, you will be able to discuss your customers' needs with them, but in a megadeal you should know them in advance.
2. Building trust and the ability to connect with different personality types is an essential sales tool. In a megadeal, building trust and mitigating risk are even more critical - and you will need to be able to do this on a large scale.
3. The ability to challenge and shift beliefs is a core competency of a megadealer, because you will need to be able to orchestrate this on a large scale, with the entire ecosystem.
4. Compelling events play a key role in traditional B2B sales. It helps to be familiar with them, but be aware that they do not play the same role in a megadeal and usually cannot be used as leverage.
5. When it comes to the people inside the selling organization that will help you win your deal, we identified what we call Trojan horses as one of the cornerstones of a megadeal. But there are many other people with critical roles to play in a deal - from the champions and the sponsors to the mobilizers. Familiarizing yourself with these types will help you be more successful in deals of any size.

6. Dialogue techniques are the basics of sales, and therefore a required skill for megadealers. You should become familiar with them, and read the literature recommended above.

CHAPTER 7

MESSAGING ARCHITECTURE

Because marketing and sales are so intertwined when it comes to mega-deals, this chapter is an important framework for both the marketing and the sales teams to understand. First and foremost, both teams need to have the same key messages.

When it comes to the key messages and related content, marketing and sometimes sales make a common mistake: they develop messaging centered around the product and supplier in an attempt to answer the question, "Why this vendor?" But organizations that are more mature when it comes to winning megadeals begin by creating messaging and content on a higher level: they create content around change drivers. This content addresses the potential buying organization's particular situation - a pain they are experiencing, current implications for their company or industry, or a compelling event, etc.

Take, for example, company X. Company X has had very little or even negative growth for a few years. To address this they may have created a key initiative called "Growth" or "Ramp-up" or something similar. You believe you have a solution to their problem: a CRM system. But that might not be the most obvious choice from their perspective. For them, the "Problem ⟶ Solution" connection is quite loose. They see many possible solutions.

So before they will be willing to discuss a CRM system with you, the company must go through a few more stages in their thinking. If they agree on the change drivers and the related problems, they might establish a list of different types of solutions or categories of solutions, such as lowering the price, adding more marketing, improving the sales strategy, implementing a new sales method, hiring 10 amazing salespeople OR buying a new CRM. This is often a long process, and in large corporations it entails an in-depth analysis that can last for many months and sometimes over a year. In this scenario, if your messaging and content is only focused on the benefits of your own CRM system, you will fail. If it is extended to also include the problems your CRM system solves, you will still underestimate and under-communicate.

Once company X has come to the conclusion that the path forward (a key initiative) includes buying and implementing a new CRM system, they then enter a process where they define what type of CRM they should buy. Should it be a cloud-based solution? Should it be integrated with the ERP system? What should the system include? Etc. This discussion can also last for a few months in a big company. When it is finished, the people at company X will start to identify which vendor(s) best fit their subcategory. I.e., "Why this vendor and not another?"

What is fundamental messaging?

To summarize, as the seller, you need to prioritize your messaging by providing support throughout the buyer's decision-making process.

There are four stages in this process:

1. What are the change drivers? (In the example above, they were "low or no growth" and the related key initiative was: "Growth" or "Ramp-up").
2. Why this category of solutions? (Why should company X solve their growth problem with a CRM system and not sales training, better

segmentation, new sales methods, adding salespeople, etc.?)
3. Why this subcategory? (Why a cloud-based CRM, or why attributes x, y, z?)
4. Why this vendor? (Now they are ready to hear the answer to "why you?" because you understand their problem, fit into their category of solution, and match the subcategory and their requirements.)

We call this "fundamental messaging" since it is fundamental to be able to back up these decision steps with convincing content.

TOP PRIORITY: FUNDAMENTAL MESSAGING - ONE PER AUDIENCE AND SOLUTION COMBINATION

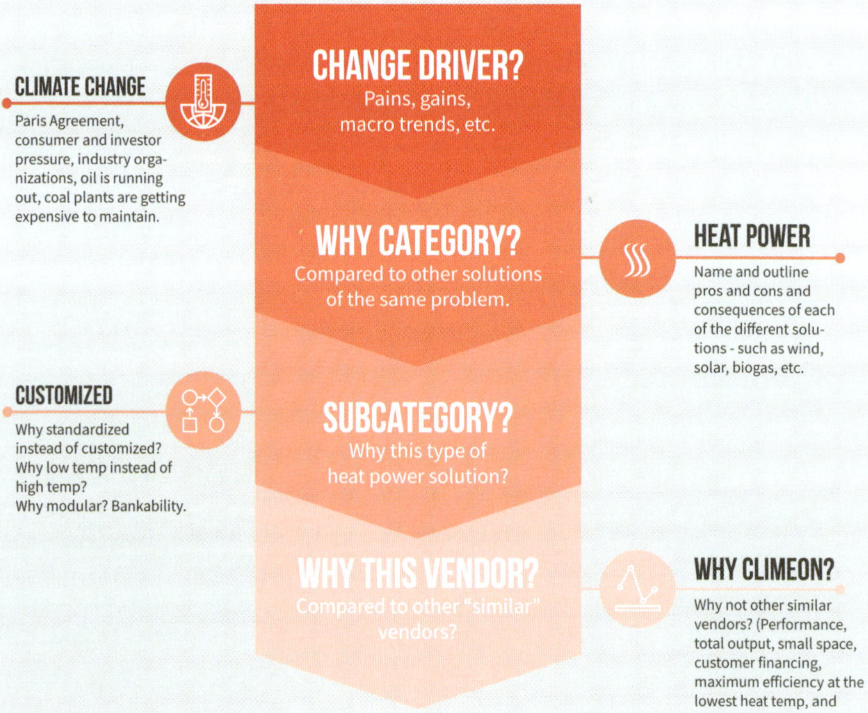

Throughout the book we are using Climeon as an example because this is one of the companies that has implemented this way of working.

There is also a risk of muddying your brand if your messages are not synchronized. Mark Stouse, CEO at Proof Analytics, often writes about how crucial it is that sales and other customer-facing teams live out what marketing says to the marketplace. "Brand reputation sums up how individual customers experience what a company says to their audience en masse," he told us.

Tailor your messages

As we discussed in Chapter 2, by mapping the stages in the megadeal decision-making process, you'll see that many small decisions are made by the various stakeholders in the ecosystem. (This mapping can be used by any B2B organization, by the way, not just for megadeals.)

So to win a megadeal, you should communicate toward accounts (we'll discuss this more in the chapter on account-based marketing). In other words, you will want to tailor your communication depending on what account you are communicating to. No matter where in the messaging architecture you are focusing.

However, it's possible that you won't know at first who the decision-makers are. Say you want to sell heat power units to the maritime industry. Do you know whether the shipyard or the ship owner signs the final contract? In fact, sometimes several parties will sign it. Or it will be unclear to you who will be doing the signing. In cases like this, you will need to direct your messaging not just at a specific person or account, but to the whole ecosystem.

What are the change drivers?

What are the fundamental causes driving change in an organization? These change drivers could be in the macro environment, or they might be specific to an industry or a company/organization. Change drivers can be either positive or negative, though in our experience they are usually negative. The client has to change. It is a must.

As the name implies, change drivers are the primary motivation for the change. They are what's driving every organization's key initiatives. We recommend using the list of examples in Chapter 1 to identify the

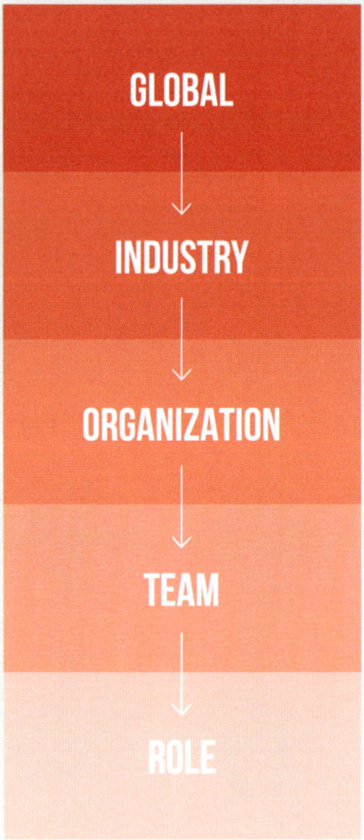

change drivers behind the key initiatives in the buying organization. This will help form the foundation for your messaging.

Change drivers come in three dimensions: global/regional, industrial and organizational. Look for a combination of two or more; this is where you will find leverage to convince the buyer to change.

Global/regional change drivers: examples

- Change in technology - electric cars
- Change in the economy - 2008 crash
- Change in the environment - climate change
- Change in competition - Spotify, Airbnb, Uber

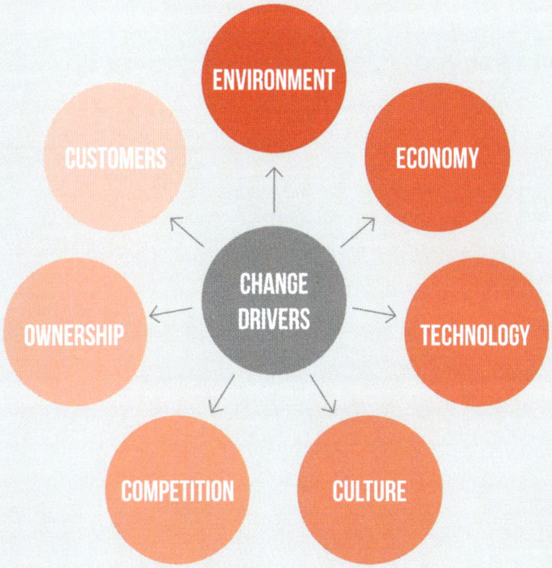

- Change in culture - downloading of music (it's considered "OK" all of a sudden to do something illegal)

Industry change drivers: examples

- Change in technology: autonomous cars
- Change in culture: ride sharing
- Change in regulations: emissions caps for the shipping industry
- Change in environment: peak amounts of a mineral or resource required to make a product work

Organizational change drivers: examples

- Change in income/profitability: The company had to issue a recall due to a parts malfunction or they had to restructure the sales force
- Change in level of growth: The last model is not selling well due to bad user experience
- Change in customer loyalty or trust: like Volkswagen after "diesel-gate," and companies that have experienced data breaches

- Reading this list, you probably noticed that many of these change drivers are interconnected. For example, changes in culture, technology, and competition are all reasons why the music industry became disrupted

But remember, just being able to identify the change will only take you so far. To succeed, you must be able to identify the motivation for those changes. Studies have shown that roughly two-thirds of the population find change difficult. So a company that decides to change is probably doing so because the alternative is even more painful than undergoing change. That pain is probably being felt on an everyday basis in the buying organization. So if, like a skilled physician, you can nail the cause of your client's pain, and describe the challenges surrounding the problem in a way that resonates with them, you will have their attention.

Believe it or not, we know of very few companies who have this messaging in place. Or if they do, the change drivers the marketing team has identified are too high level. Because of this, the sales team won't use the messaging. They will instead develop their own, and start from zero again.

Why this category out of the possible solutions?

The change drivers are the fundamental challenges or opportunities that the category you represent can help solve. However, like in our example of company X above, the category you represent is probably one of several possible solutions to the buyer's problem.

That's why, at this level of the messaging architecture, the goal is to separate your category of solution from other categories that you're competing with. It is important not to communicate as if you are a business, but rather as a journalist. A journalist would compare across categories.

The core messages here should therefore answer the question: "Why this category?" Where many companies and marketers fall short is that they skip to the bottom of the messaging architecture and instead answer the question: "Why us?" or "Why our product?" This is a big mistake.

The goal of the messaging architecture is to make it easy for your sales

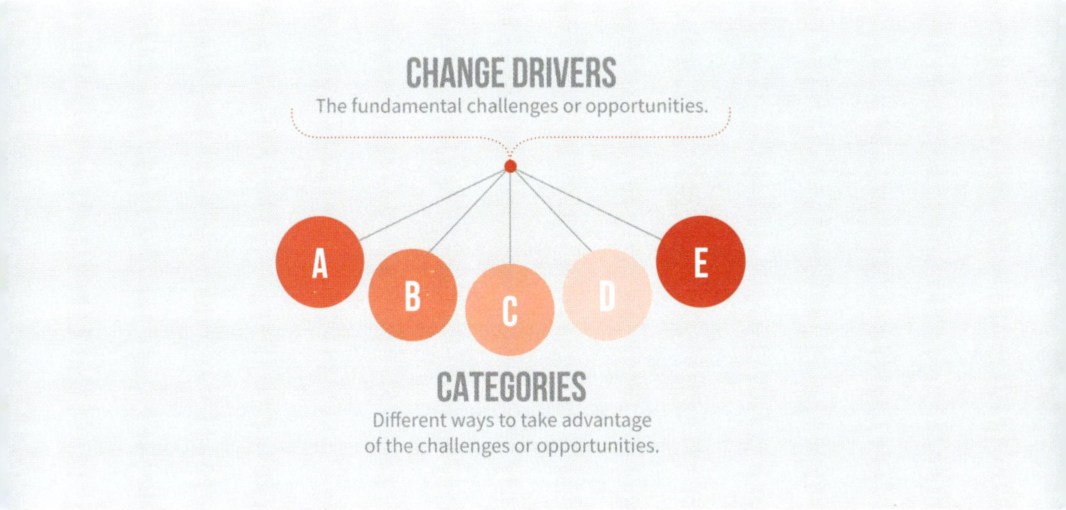

and marketing team to structure their communication. By knowing which other categories of solutions you are competing with, you can create messages with a level of detail that is easy to work with, and that help you create great communication and content. Don't overcomplicate it.

Here's an example. Let's say you sell electric buses. The city of Paris is considering ways to handle the growing number of people who enter and exit the city each day. They could solve this volume problem in a number of ways. They could incentivize biking, refurbish the subway system and/or add lines, widen roads for more car traffic, create carpool incentives - or extend and improve their bus system.

Example of the land transportation category:

Category of solutions	Bus, subway, car, bicycle, etc.
Subcategory	Electric buses

As an electric bus manufacturer, examples of themes for your communication pieces around land transportation in the "Why this category of solutions?" stage could be:

1. Why expanding the bus network would cost less than refurbishing the city's subway system

2. New subway, autonomous buses, electric bicycles, and drones? How will Paris's transportation evolve over the next 20 years?
3. The 10 cities with the happiest commuters

Why your subcategory?

A subcategory is a part of your category with special attributes. In the example above, an electric bus is one subcategory. The others would be gas/diesel-powered buses, ethanol-powered buses, or autonomous buses. No matter what you are selling, your offering fits into a subcategory within the category of solutions to the customer's problem.

The goal for your communication here is to clarify why your subcategory is more relevant and a better choice than the other subcategories. Your business can, of course, be part of several subcategories. You might specialize in autonomous buses *and* electric buses.

Once you begin communicating with your potential customers within the subcategory (instead of communicating directly to them as a vendor), you get to shape the discussion. Having identified your customer's change drivers and pain point, your opinion of the subcategory will be seen as educational. And as a thought leader, you can sell like crazy without anyone realizing it. Just be sure to stay neutral and objective, and give credit to other subcategories of solutions (biofuel buses may be ideal for cross-country bus transport, for example). When correctly executed, this will feel objective to the client rather than salesy, and you will therefore increase trust.

For the electric bus manufacturer, examples of themes for communication pieces in the "Why this subcategory?" stage would be:

1. Electric vs. diesel vs. ethanol: how these choices affect the environment in the short-term and long-term
2. Five major reasons why fossil-free buses are not enough (biogas, for example, still creates exhaust and noise)
3. Electric buses can save local governments billions. Just look at China.

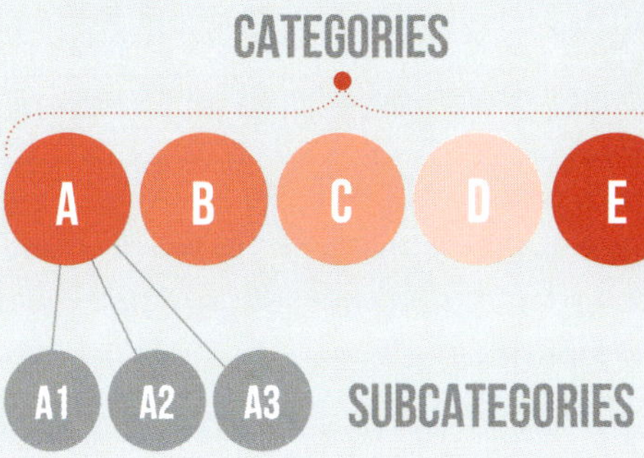

Why this vendor? (I.e., Why you?)

While it is necessary to answer the question of "Why this vendor?", most marketers place too much focus on this type of messaging. The purpose of your communication at this stage is to differentiate your offering from that of your competitors.

In many situations, if you have followed the messaging architecture, creating content around "Why this vendor?" will not even be necessary - because you have already out-positioned your competition in your messaging on "Why this subcategory?" In fact, we know of one company that adopted this framework, used it to out-position the competition and even claimed to have doubled their revenue because of it! By distancing yourself from the competition on the subcategory level, you are making the decision easier for the buyer: they move straight to "Why you?" because no one else is in your subcategory.

Examples of themes for communication pieces for land transportation for an electric bus manufacturer in the "Why Vendor":

1. Are you working with a company that shares your corporate values? (I.e., why it matters to choose an electric bus maker that wants to slow climate change)

2. Key features to look for in an electric bus
3. How loud is your electric bus?
4. Charge your electric buses with a fast-charging system (time is money)

Typically, sales messaging around “Why this vendor?” focuses on a company’s value propositions, benefits and features. However, we recommend that you first communicate your company values and then address benefits and features.

As Simon Sinek said in his famous TED Talk, “People don’t buy what you do, they buy why you do it.” It is significantly more powerful when you communicate “Why this vendor” from the inside out, as Sinek illustrates using his Golden Circle model. In other words, start by arguing for why you make electric buses before getting into what’s so special about your bus.

Values are so important in megadeals that they can be what differentiates you on the subcategory level. More and more companies are asking for a declaration of values in their RFPs, and certain companies are quite open about the fact that they do not work with companies who do not share their values. Apple, for example, has pledged to use only renewable energy, a decision that has had a ripple effect on its suppliers.

Because a megadeal usually results in a long-running relationship, shared values are an indication of long-term compatibility. Those relationships will by default have conflicts, but if you and your buyer share the same values, you are more likely to resolve them amicably. (David Frydlinger addresses this in depth in his chapter on contracts.)

For each of the four layers about Change drivers, Why category, Why subcategory and Why this vendor, you can create battle cards that cover all the relevant options on levels 2-4 of the messaging architecture.
By hosting workshops and training around the options on those three levels, sales will be more synchronized and sharper. New marketing and sales people will also onboard faster.

With your messaging in place, your sales and marketing teams can begin to use it in different contexts, from social selling to PR. This ensures that everyone on the selling team is prepared with the same intelligence. Plus, since research has proven that repeated messages are more effective, you will increase your likelihood of cutting through the clutter and actually being heard.

Your fundamental messaging is the first piece in your messaging architecture. The next two are deal-closing messaging and orientational messaging.

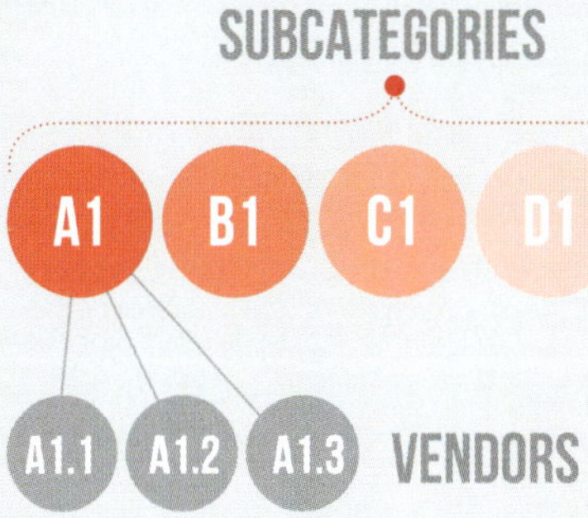

Deal-closing messaging

When the stakeholders have mentally gone through the four decision steps (Change drivers, Why this category, Why this subcategory and Why this vendor) in the messaging architecture, it should be evident that you are the right vendor. But before they will actually sign on the dotted line, more small decisions will need to be made and many matters will need to be clarified.

The type of messaging you should be crafting at this time is what we call deal-closing messaging. These are messages centered around how to go from a vendor decision to signing, from signing to going live, from launch to a relationship. You will also need messaging around risk mitigation and consensus creation. As we stated in the first part of the book, risk mitigation and consensus creation are cornerstones of a megadeal. As with your other messaging, you will have a higher win rate if you have prepared your messages in advance. Sure, the content you create will be slightly different from case to case, but you can always customize your messages - and that's a lot better than starting from zero.

Deal-closing messaging consists of three types

1. "How" messaging

The purpose of "how" messaging is to make clear what needs to happen from a mental yes to an actual signing. It covers three sequential phases:

A. How do you move the customer from the feeling of wanting to buy from you to actually signing a contract? What needs to happen and who does what from that point until signing?
B. How do you go from signing a contract to going live?
C. How will the ongoing relationship work? SLAs, who does what? Who will be the main contact as you move forward? How do the spare parts work? What happens when small orders are added to the overall contract?

All of this is important because you are communicating with a lot of different people from surrounding organizations in a megadeal. The above questions and how messaging are relevant only for a small group of people who are directly involved on a day-to-day basis.

2. Risk mitigation messaging

As we discussed in Chapter 5, mitigating risk is a cornerstone of a successful megadeal. Yet it's something most B2B marketers are clueless about because it is not that important in traditional B2B marketing. There are two types of messaging you need for risk mitigation: messages that work to establish trust, and messages that demonstrate why the external risks are low.

First, you should craft messaging that develops trust in:

A. Your category
B. Your subcategory
C. Your company
D. Your offering
E. Your people

Communication is, of course, only one part of establishing trust, but it is a great tool when you need to do this at scale. You can communicate trust through reference cases, interviews with the team, showing performance compared with that of competitors or with that of other subcategories, etc. Remember to make your risk mitigation content account-based and tailored. This is not general information to be posted on your website.

Mitigating risks involves more than just establishing trust. Rember, a risk is anything that can happen that should not happen, or something that did not happen that should have happened.

When creating deal-closing content around risk mitigation, it is therefore also important to analyze what risks the buyers think can occur, and then create messaging that shows how those can be mitigated. (It will help to refer here to Chapter 5, where we review examples of real and perceived risks.)

3. Consensus creation

The third type of deal-closing messaging is focused around creating consensus within the ecosystem. This involves condensing all four layers of the fundamental messaging into content that can be easily shared, such as a short video and/or a slide deck that can be used for lobby conversations. This type of content should also be available on your website, and in the LinkedIn profiles of everyone on your team.

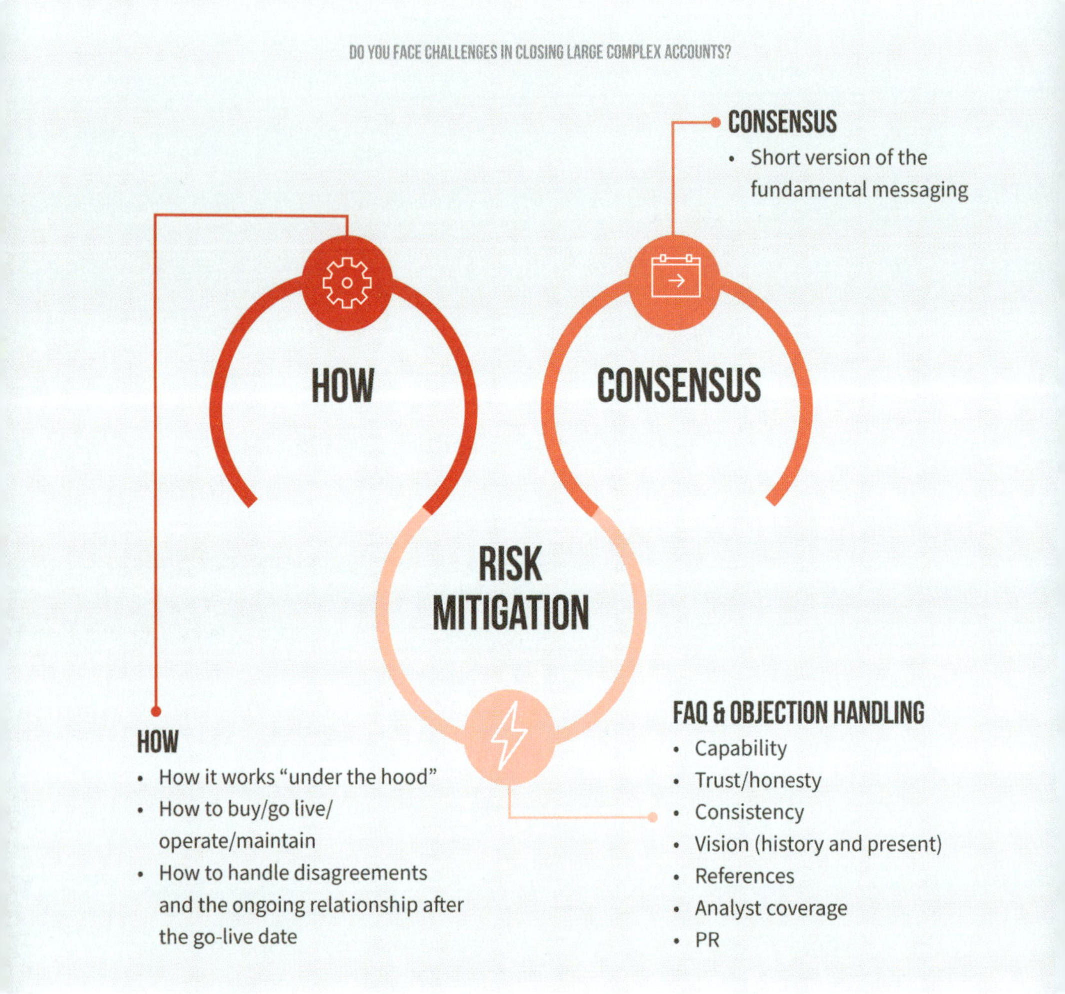

Orientational messaging

Have you ever seen a James Bond movie? Of course you have. Ever thought about the Aston Martin in the movie? They have been part of countless Bond movies, but they have never been the star of the show. Orientational messaging is similar. It takes a bigger approach than just your category or subcategory. Because it takes a bigger perspective, your audience will be interested even though they are not interested in you.

Orientational messaging has two main purposes:

A. To capture the interest of people/companies that have not yet expressed interest in your category or subcategory, i.e. lead generation.
B. To nurture and build trust among potential and existing clients that are not in a "buying mood."

Let's take megadeals as an example. We can probably assume that you're interested in megadeals because you are reading this book, right? But for a second, let's imagine that you're not interested in megadeals, but that you are a C-level executive. We might create a video, article, webinar or seminar themed "The five major pitfalls for growth for the Fortune 1000 until 2020." In the communication piece, one of the pitfalls would be the risk of getting stuck in transactional selling.

If your marketing and sales team is good at orientational content, there is a much higher chance that you will be able to shape the ecosystem. This skill of being able to see the bigger picture and even predict where it will lead is a master skill among megadealers.

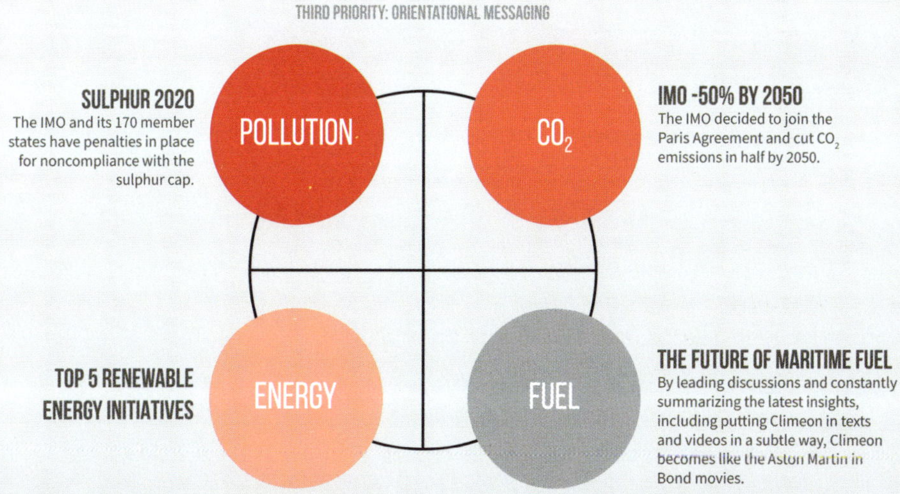

An example of Climeon's orientational messaging.

The messaging architecture summarized

The messaging architecture can be summarized with this illustration:

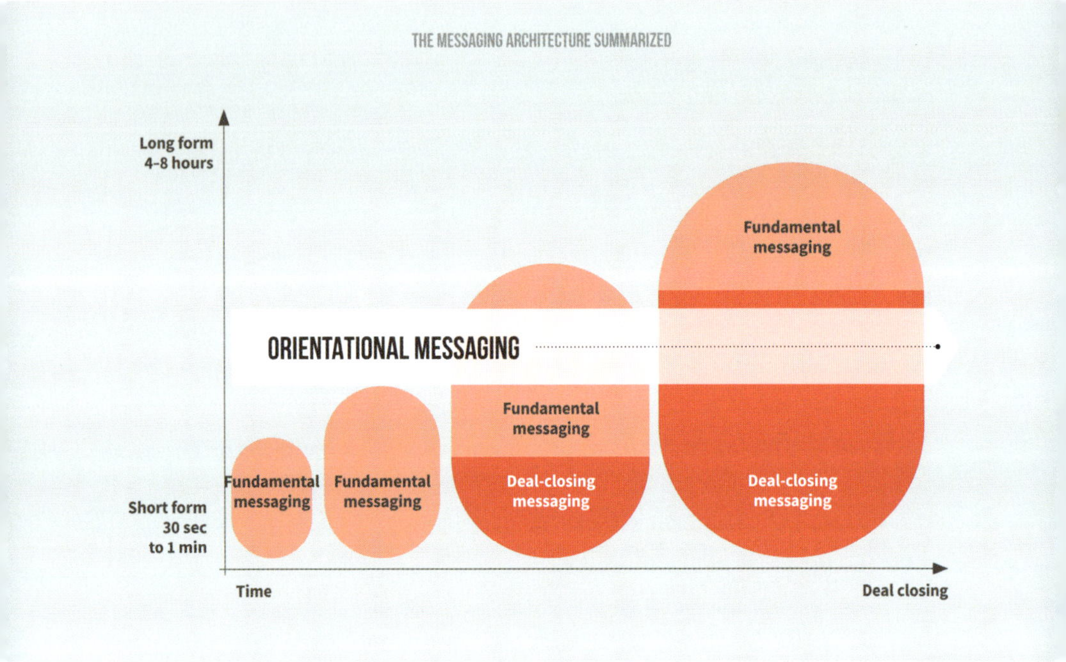

Time, depth and iterations

How should you think about the length and depth of your messaging and related content? The buyer will, in the beginning, spend most of her/his time (which is probably not that much time) in level 1-3 of the messaging architecture above (Change drivers, Why category, Why subcategory). As the buying journey progresses, you will need to produce more extensive and deeper content. The format or media does not matter - it could be a video, a presentation, an article, etc.

How much time they spend with the messaging on each level will depend on market maturity, but buyers will go through all four. Failing to produce great messaging in all four categories of the architecture is a common mistake. As we've mentioned previously, most companies skip the category and subcategory messaging.

A big difference between megadeals and traditional B2B sales is that there are a lot of stakeholders involved. Both in terms of direct stakeholders and in terms of the extended target group. This means that not everyone has the same A) amount of information B) attitude towards the deal C) interest in spending time on or the possibility of seeing your content.

So at any given point in time, all four categories of fundamental messaging are needed, but different people will consume different content at different lengths and depths. We categorize this consumption as lightweight, mediumweight, and heavyweight.

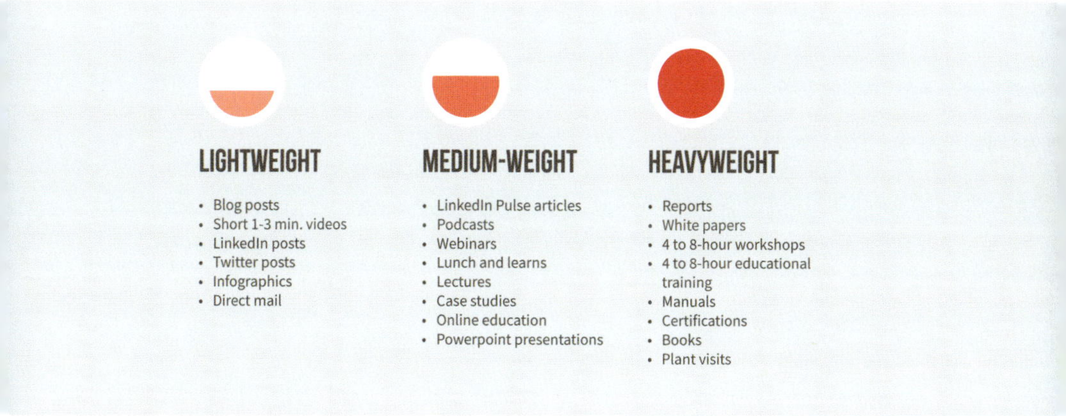

The power of human emotion

A common mistake in B2B corporate messaging, no matter what the media, is failing to connect with human emotion. We have heard over and over and over again that we are in B2B, not B2C. Yes, and no. We don't like the expression B2H or H2H - as in business to human, or human to human. That's because the way you strategically market your offering, especially in a megadeal, is very different from B2C and even traditional B2B.

How should you use emotional messaging and what are good examples?

- Standalone emotional messaging.
- Emotional messaging incorporated into other messaging.

You should work with standalone emotional messaging that communicates company values and how they relate to behaviors, including real-life examples. Another typically strong type of emotional messaging can be centered around the story of your company. It can also be strengthened by stories about individuals, WHY they work at your company, and how they feel about contributing to a better world. However, you should still try to include snippets of emotional messaging in all your communication.

We have learned a few things about what makes content attractive:

1. It should be challenging, educational and entertaining.
2. It should be real and authentic.
3. Think outside-in on the fundamental messaging, the deal-closing messaging and the orientational messaging.
4. Videos are more interesting than text. If you use text, make sure to have good photos or illustrations. Pure text is rarely engaging enough.
5. Short content typically gets consumed more than long content (a lot of what gets consumed the most takes less than two minutes to watch, read, etc.).
6. Wherever possible, add a cute cat in your photos. ;-)

One last overall comment on this chapter is that you are probably using everything we've mentioned here all the time - regardless of whether you have intentionally prepared these messages or not. Every day that passes while you continue to use them on an ad hoc basis is a loss for your marketing and sales since the quality will be lower. Also, it will take more time to handle each step because you're having to start from scratch in every situation. Quality will increase and time spent will decrease if you can find a way to work on it jointly in a reusable format (Excel is not a bad start, nor is Google docs).

To quote Mark Ogne, the Founder and CEO of ABM Consortium, "Trust can also come from the consistency of your content strategy. Are you making it easy for your customers to buy and understand what it is you are trying to sell? If so, they will ultimately trust you as a source."

EXERCISES

Exercise #1

- What are the top three global macro change drivers affecting your most important clients?
- What are the top three industry change drivers affecting your most important clients?
- What are the top three organizational change drivers affecting your most important clients?
- How will you implement these change drivers in your sales and marketing?

Exercise #2:

- Which are the top 3-5 categories you are competing with today? What about in 3 years?
- What are the strengths and weaknesses of your category of solution? What are the strengths and weaknesses of the competing 3-5 categories?
- What are titles or themes for communication pieces that could address the question, "Why our category of solutions?"

> "ARE YOU MAKING IT EASY FOR YOUR CUSTOMERS TO BUY AND UNDERSTAND WHAT IT IS YOU ARE TRYING TO SELL? IF SO, THEY WILL ULTIMATELY TRUST YOU AS A SOURCE."

Exercise #3:

- Which are the top 1-3 subcategories you are competing with today? How about in 3 years?
- What are the strengths and weaknesses of your subcategory compared to the top 3-5 other subcategories?
- What are titles or themes for communication pieces that would answer the question, "Why this subcategory?"

Exercise #4:

- Which are the top 1-3 vendors you are competing with today? In 3 years?
- What are the strengths and weaknesses of your business compared to the competition's?
- What are titles or themes for communication pieces that would answer the question, "Why this vendor?" ("Why us?")
- Consider doing battle cards for each competitor, so you have ready messages for different situations, and responses for every argument.

Final exercise

1. Run a workshop per segment and look at what messaging and content you have and don't have for each layer in the fundamental messaging, deal-closing content and orientational messaging. What are your biggest gaps? Book sessions to set the messaging for each level. Start with the Excel matrix.
2. Evaluate which parts of the messaging architecture should be covered by sales, marketing or both. Hint: The vast majority should be covered by both groups.
3. Start producing related content in both short and long form. Make sure you cover content that addresses your fundamental messaging first and that you start with the short formats.

KEY TAKEAWAYS

1. Buyers go through many more decision-making steps than just Problem → Solution.
2. Add messaging around why the customer should use your category of solution for the designated problem and not a substitute. Think CRM vs. sales training, for example. Most people forget to sell their category. You might think that the customer is comparing you with your competition, while in reality they are evaluating a few completely different categories of solutions (or subcategories).
3. Add messaging around why the subcategory you represent is better than other subcategories. Think online CRM with a ready-made ERP integration vs. an installed CRM software with features x, y, z. A Climeon example is that heat power has subcategories, such as large, customized high-temperature engines and Climeon is a low-temperature, standardized and modular solution.
4. Creating consensus and risk mitigation are cornerstones of a successful megadeal that require specific messaging. Risk mitigation requires its own type of content while your messaging for consensus creation will involve condensing the fundamental messaging (all four layers) down to, for example, a short video and/or a slide deck that can be used for lobby conversations.

CHAPTER 8

ENTERPRISE SOCIAL SELLING

"People do business with people." We heard this over and over again in our interviews with megadealers.

As we mentioned in Chapter 5, Johan Bjorklund was behind one of the biggest deals in telecom history. He was so detailed in his approach to social selling that his team created a giant spreadsheet that they tacked onto the wall every day.

"On the y-axis, it included everyone we interfaced with on the client side - roughly 100 people," Bjorklund recalled. "On the x-axis, we wrote down what we knew about them: their recreational interests, favorite sports team, where they went to school, you name it. Each night we took it down, updated it, then reposted it the next day. There were 150 of us on the selling team, and each one of us was matched according to interest so that if we had a meeting, we knew who to bring and how to engage everyone there."

This deal was signed in 2009. Today, tools like LinkedIn make Johan Björklund's spreadsheet look like something out of the Flintstones. But if you follow our advice, you'll still have the same results.

"Strong friendships were forged during this process," Bjorklund added, "because we weren't just trying to sell something - we were building long-term relationships."

> WE WEREN'T JUST TRYING TO SELL SOMETHING - WE WERE BUILDING LONG-TERM RELATIONSHIPS."

What is social selling?
During the past few years, social selling as a method of traditional selling has experienced a boom thanks to innovation and the resulting digitalization. However, there are still a lot of misconceptions out there about what social selling is, how to use it and what positive effects it can have on your team's sales. Social selling is simply about using social media as an individual and a team to reach sales outcomes, just like Johan Bjorklund did.

In this chapter, we will give you details on how to use social selling to:

1. Create a map of the stakeholders and decision makers (the deal ecosystem from Chapter 2) at the companies you are going after.
2. Build awareness, confidence and trust at scale towards your stakeholders, influencers and decision makers.
3. Establish initial contact and get appointments with the right stakeholders and decision makers.

Our main focus in this chapter is LinkedIn, but the ideas will work on most social media platforms.

When pursuing a megadeal, there are five core problems that social selling can solve:
1. Mapping the right stakeholders and decision makers is difficult.
In our research, we have found that it is common to have up to 200-300 stakeholders and decision panels of up to 30-50 people. Mapping these stakeholders can be painful for your sales team.

2. Former methods for initiating contact are outdated.
Today, decision makers and key people are bombarded with phone calls and emails. (One C-level executive we spoke to said he received over 400 new emails every day.) As a consequence, these people generally do not pick up the phone and may be screening calls with apps such as Truecaller (which works like a really big phone book). Nor do they answer emails. The challenge for your sales team is to find ways to establish contact.

3. Too much direct communication tires the potential client.
People receive too much information every day. To cut through the clutter, it is important to communicate over and over and over again. The problem is, if you reach out directly to your clients too frequently, it will create fatigue. This may lessen their trust in you, your company and colleagues, and the receivers become less likely to want to consume your message. In the end, they will be less likely to engage and buy from you.

4. It is difficult to build trust at scale.
As discussed at length in Chapter 5, trust is a key component in mitigating risk. Building trust at scale is difficult because trust in most cases is both personal and organizational. You might think that it is impossible to build trust online, that it has to be face to face. Later in this chapter we will show how you can use social selling as an important part of building trust at scale.

To quote Mark Stouse again, "In social selling, trust is not usually a function of what you post. It's the consistency and integrity of what you post, and it's impacted heavily by how you respond to other people's comments."

5. It is time-consuming to influence a large number of people.
One of the most common mistakes we see people make when trying to win a megadeal is that they concentrate the efforts of their sales team on too few key people on the client side. Their reasons often have to do with lack of time or laziness, and also because they are afraid of upsetting key relationships. However, this can unfortunately delay or sabotage the entire deal or account.

Five steps to effective social selling

We find that most people in senior positions (yes, the people leading megadeals usually hold senior positions) make pretty basic errors because they typically think social media won't help them. They say they want to focus on doing real business. They are not seeing the forest for the trees. Especially in megadeals, you need to reach deep into an organization, build trust at scale and get many people to say yes. For this, there is no better tool than social media. The key words here are "trust" and "at scale."

Get your profile ready for social selling (LinkedIn)

Get the basics right. If you have extensive experience in social selling, some of these guidelines might be too basic for you. If so, move past the profile, but remember, like most things in life, to succeed you must first master the basics.

1. Photo

Have a professionally taken photo and preferably a background photo as well.

2. Headline

The full profile headline will appear in searches and when you send contact requests. A bad headline will decrease both trust and conversion rate for new and relevant contacts.

Make the headline compelling and make sure to build trust. Here are two examples: Johan Aberg and Christopher Engman's profile head-

lines prominently feature their titles, businesses, and that they are the authors of *Megadeals*.

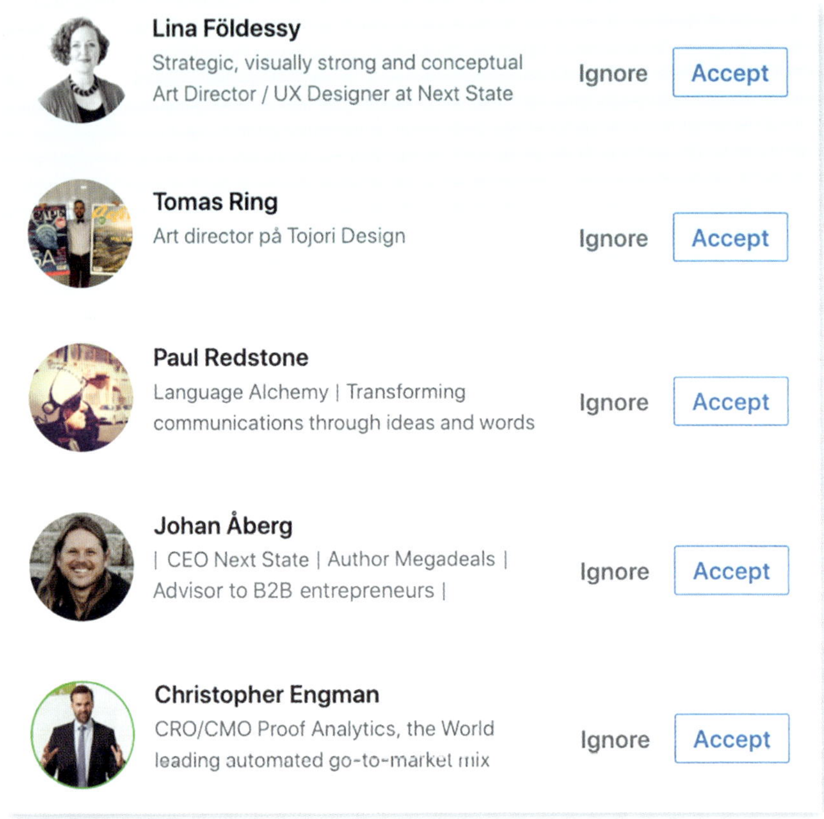

3. Profile text

We have a complete chapter on how to formulate messaging because it is really important in several key areas. Go to Chapter 6 to take a deep dive into messaging.

A great profile text has three building blocks:

Building block 1:
A general text for the team that focuses on major pains of the clients and segment that the team is pursuing. Go to Chapter 6 for details of how to build your message and see the examples shown here from Johan and Christopher's profiles.

Building block 2:
A short description of your personal strengths and profile.

Building block 3:
Call to action and contact information such as phone, email and preferred contact method.

See Johan and Christopher's updated profiles here

www.linkedin.com/in/johanaaberg/

www.linkedin.com/in/christopherengman/

If you have any suggestions for improvements or special insights, please add us on LinkedIn and send us a message!

The most common mistake we see in LinkedIn profiles is that they are written from an inside-out perspective. People typically write something like: "I am a highly motivated results-focused CRO with a strong track record within the technology sector."

Zzzzz. That kind of text just sounds like any old CV. Be better than that. Write about what is important to your clients, i.e., their pains, challenges, struggles and success cases.

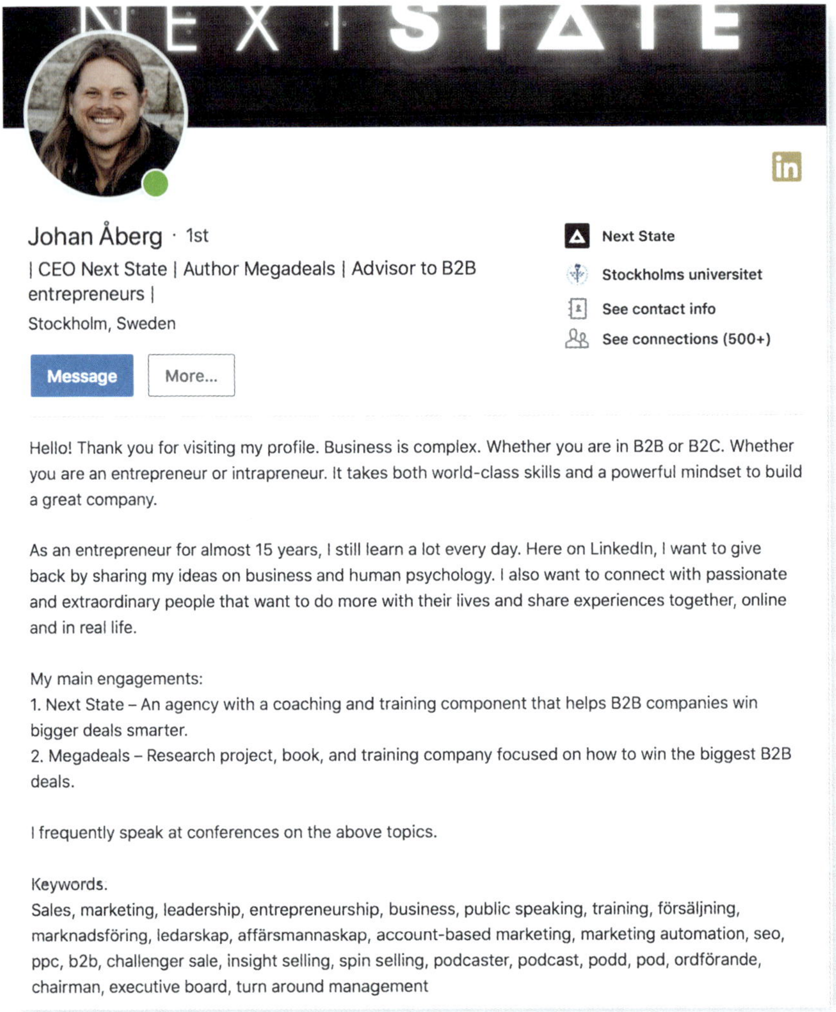

Johan Åberg · 1st

| CEO Next State | Author Megadeals | Advisor to B2B entrepreneurs |

Stockholm, Sweden

Message More...

Next State

Stockholms universitet

See contact info

See connections (500+)

Hello! Thank you for visiting my profile. Business is complex. Whether you are in B2B or B2C. Whether you are an entrepreneur or intrapreneur. It takes both world-class skills and a powerful mindset to build a great company.

As an entrepreneur for almost 15 years, I still learn a lot every day. Here on LinkedIn, I want to give back by sharing my ideas on business and human psychology. I also want to connect with passionate and extraordinary people that want to do more with their lives and share experiences together, online and in real life.

My main engagements:
1. Next State – An agency with a coaching and training component that helps B2B companies win bigger deals smarter.
2. Megadeals – Research project, book, and training company focused on how to win the biggest B2B deals.

I frequently speak at conferences on the above topics.

Keywords.
Sales, marketing, leadership, entrepreneurship, business, public speaking, training, försäljning, marknadsföring, ledarskap, affärsmannaskap, account-based marketing, marketing automation, seo, ppc, b2b, challenger sale, insight selling, spin selling, podcaster, podcast, podd, pod, ordförande, chairman, executive board, turn around management

Do you know what creates the most value and what generates the least? How long does it take to realize ROI? Proof transforms your data and KPIs into computed portraits of attribution and correlated value. There many types of analytics tools, but no one delivers proof of value like Proof.

Christopher Engman • 2nd

CRO/CMO Proof Analytics, the World leading automated go-to-market mix modeling solution | Speaker | Author Megadeals |

Djursholm, Stockholm County, Sweden

Proof Analytics

Luleå University of Technology

See contact info

500+ connections

Message

More...

Proof (www.proofanalytics.ai) answers three of the main questions CEOs, CFOs, CROs, and CMOs have about their go-to-market work.

1. How should we balance the costs between sales and marketing?
2. Which of my marketing categories should we increase, decrease, add or take away?
3. How do the various marketing and sales activities contribute to revenue, profit, and cash flow?

Proof bridges the ROI gap between CMOs and CFOs, delivering cause-and-effect analytics that show the business impact and financial value of marketing and sales.

Megadeals
The first book about megadeals is finally here. (www.megadealsadvisory.com)

What is a megadeal?
A megadeal has four core attributes:
- A deal size from 10 MUSD to 15 BUSD (could be larger but we haven't found one)
- High to ultra-high complexity (not just in terms of the solution, which is often written about in sales books)
- The deal often contains a mix of hardware, software and services
- Change management is involved

Some of the main insights:
- If your offer does not align with your customer's key initiatives, it is almost impossible to find the money for your megadeal.
- Without an understanding of or the ability to influence the ecosystem around the deal, you will not close the deal. In most cases, there are more than 100 relevant stakeholders.
- Megadeals per definition involve a lot of risk. The ability to control and mitigate those risks, rather than just maximizing the upside, is a key capability - and it is barely discussed in most sales and marketing literature.
- For a deeper dive, attend a Megadeals seminar, 2-day training or read the book.

Because of their size, scope, complexity, and status, megadeals are deeply meaningful to the megadealers behind them. They present an opportunity to change the world for the better on a massive scale.

4. Experience and education

This is not a super-important section of the profile. But make sure that you at least fill in the most important positions you have had as well as your education.

5. Improve the branding of your profile (optional)

Depending on your brand, your current position/role and the opportunities you have available, there is great power in branding. There are several ways you can do this on LinkedIn:

- Recommendations from credible people
- Pulse articles that raise your credibility
- Third-party appearances such as mentions in newspapers, etc.

Build your network

For obvious reasons, social selling will not work if you don't have the right network. It's like standing in an empty bar trying to talk to interesting people; it's just not going to work.

In the chapter on ABM, we go in-depth into client segmentation. Let's make a simple calculation to define how you should look at your network.

Number of prioritized accounts	Number of key stakeholders and decision makers per account	Number of influencers/ extended target group per account	The total target group for social selling
100	30	250	30,000

Depending on the number of accounts and the penetration you need in each account, the network size will vary from 1,000 to 30,000 people.

In the extended target group, also include important people outside the buying organization. Key steps:

1. Decide who from your team should be part of this effort (it should be at least 5 people).
2. Decide which accounts to focus on.
3. Create a well-written text to connect with new connections.
4. Add the key stakeholders.
5. Add the extended target group.

Make sure that you have at least 10 mutual connections to the people you add. People are more likely to accept requests if you have mutual connections.

A personal message will get you a higher response rate. For important connections, make sure to personalize the message. But before you connect, please start with bee swarming.

Bee swarming

Bee swarming is a really simple yet effective approach that is easy to implement. LinkedIn has a feature that most people have used, "Who's viewed your profile" and, as you can guess if you haven't used it, you can see who has viewed your profile. People tend to be curious about who has viewed their profile.

There are five main reasons why bee swarming is really effective:

1. The barrier to entry is low. You don't need to spend a lot of time and effort to produce content. You just have to have a great profile.
2. People have egos and are curious. We want to know who looked at our profile.
3. Big companies have complex matrix organizations, and by influencing many people in those organizations, we reduce the risk of overlooking key stakeholders.
4. As discussed in Chapter 5, large companies are heavily focused on risk mitigation, and large financial decisions involve a lot of people in that process.

BEE SWARMING

Directed at a vast number of stakeholders, including the key stakeholders. Bee swarming entails visiting the LinkedIn profiles of the stakeholders you want to later connect with on LinkedIn and eventually have calls/meetings with.

5. With bee swarming you can get attention from 30+ people per account without consuming a lot of time and resources.

Big companies are usually matrix organizations. Because of this, communicating with stakeholders is often resource intensive and time-consuming. Here is how we recommend going about it:

- Visit the profiles of people with whom you have first, second and third-hand connections who are key stakeholders or in your extended target group.
- Visiting these profiles once every 1-2 months is a good rate.
- Make sure that you have at least 3-5 people in your team working with bee swarming around the same accounts. This will supercharge the effect. A common reaction is: "Five people from X company have been looking at my profile. Are they trying to hire me or are they talking about me?"

LinkedIn Sales Navigator is the world's best research tool

Sales Navigator in LinkedIn has a world-class search function. It's extremely effective to map an account because almost everyone in a senior position at a large enterprise has a LinkedIn account. If you are not currently using Sales Navigator, just start. It is going to pay off. The search function is by far the most valuable part of Sales Navigator. To give you an idea of how it works, here's a screen shot of the Advanced Lead Search function in LinkedIn's Sales Navigator.

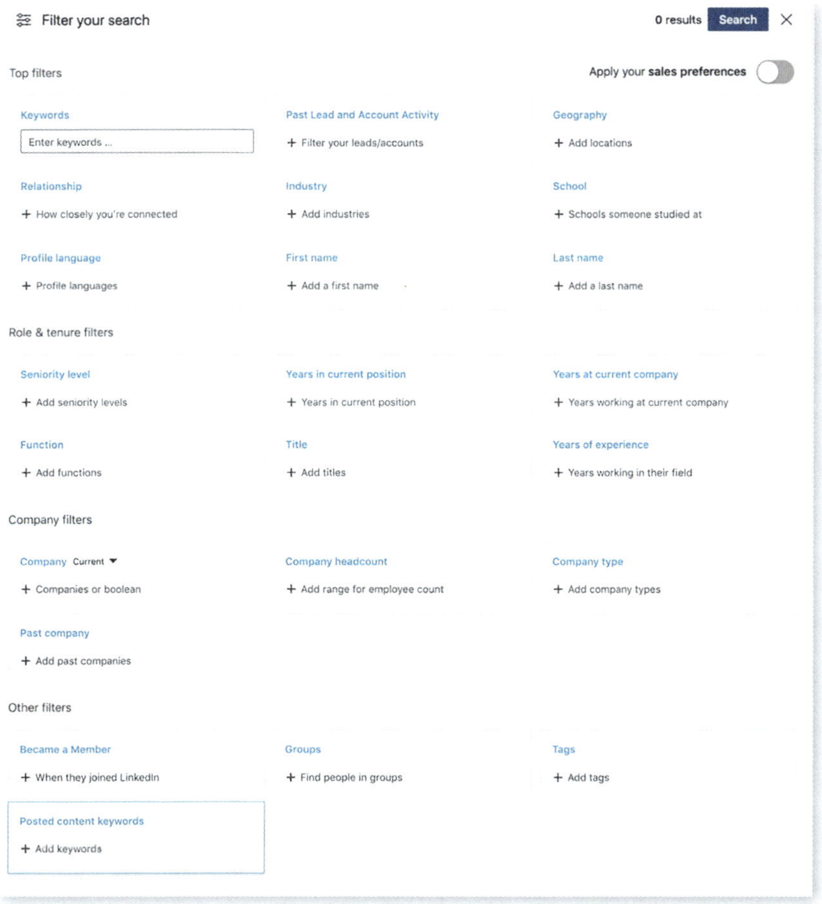

World-class content and posts

Great content is a significant part of using LinkedIn as a social selling tool in megadeals. It is still easy to get your message in front of your most important accounts. LinkedIn is like Facebook was in the beginning; it is easy to create reach. This will most likely change over time. Depending on when you are reading this, perhaps it already has changed!

Because we have an entire chapter on how to create a great message there will be some repetition, but this is very important for success, so read carefully.

We recommend using LinkedIn posts, but there is also a publishing function called LinkedIn Pulse. In general, Pulse articles do not get at all the same traction as posts. The reason is most likely that LinkedIn wants people to post more regularly to make people visit the platform more frequently. That said, Pulse articles are important when someone starts to research you. And, unlike posts, articles don't vanish after a while.

Simple content guidelines for LinkedIn

Go to Chapter 7 to dive deeply into how to craft and structure your messaging.

Challenge:

Create posts that challenge their current reality and their beliefs. If you are communicating the obvious, you will lose credibility. Instead, if you can change their beliefs about what is true, you will gain trust and respect.

Educate:

Create posts that educate your audience about their problems, pains, and struggles, as well as trends and advice on how to achieve their desired outcomes.

Entertain:

Create posts that entertain and emotionally connect you and your brand with your audience.

Depending on your audience, your personality and your brand, you might want to adjust the mix of your posts.

DECIDE THE MIX FOR YOUR TEAM'S POSTS

What should the relationship between educating, challenging and entertaining be?

Challenge	(1) ├──────────┤ (5)
Educate	(1) ├──────────┤ (5)
Entertain	(1) ├──────────┤ (5)

How often should you post?

We currently recommend two or three LinkedIn posts per week. Focus on increasing the quality and the interactions in the comments in the posts rather than on posting a lot of content.

Video

Video is a powerful tool on LinkedIn. It's 20 times more likely to be shared than other content on the platform.

There are two types of videos we recommend for LinkedIn - both have the same base:

- Video length: 3-10 minutes (LinkedIn has a max length of 10 minutes). Note that shorter videos are more likely to be watched to the end, but long films can be just as successful as short ones if they contain great content.
- Shoot with a professional videographer who also acts as a sidekick in the video.
- Use "one take" and jump cuts (i.e., not too many retakes).
- Talk about topics that are interesting to your target accounts, not just your product or service.
- Shoot in interesting locations, not just a boring office.

Video type 1 - Talk into the camera:
Talk right into the camera.

Example: Johan shares five major marketing mistakes.

Video type 2 - Interview interesting people:
Use branding by association if possible, by interviewing people that your target accounts will find interesting and trustworthy.

Use an interview setting (so the subjects are looking off-camera and don't need to talk right into the camera, which is new to many and can be uncomfortable for some).

Example: Johan interviews his and Christopher's friend Navin Thukkaram.

It is also important to remember to set your own tone of voice. If you have watched Next State's videos, you might say, "I am in the XYZ business. This is too entertaining for me." Remember to adjust the tone according to how you or your brand want to be perceived in terms of educating, challenging and entertaining.

Example: In this compelling use of storytelling, David Klättborg explains how a previous career prepared him for his current one. Transition stories can be especially useful for new people on your team.

More examples

How Automated Marketing Mix Modeling (AMMM) Can Help Your Business Grow Faster and Be More Profitable

Published on April 9, 2019

Christopher Engman
CRO/CMO Proof Analytics, the World leading automated go-to-market mix mo... See more

21 articles + Follow

Optimizing your go-to-market mix

If you work at a medium-sized or large corporation (B2B or B2C), optimizing your go-to-market mix could be the fastest way to increase revenue, cash-flow and/or profitability. Even outsourcing a function or building a new factory is unlikely to have as much immediate and significant financial impact as having a powerful tool like Proof.

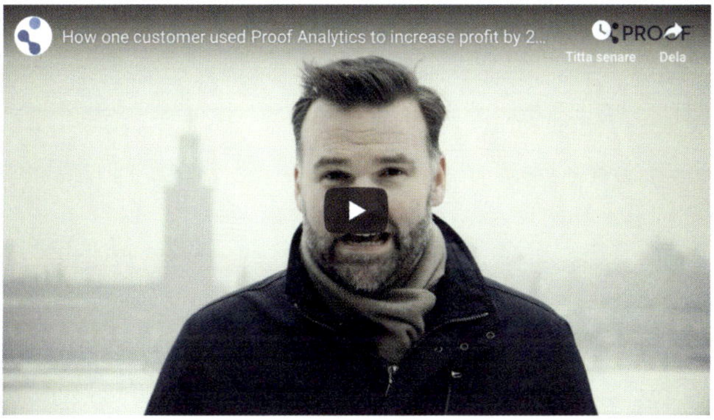

One of our early users, a global $2B enterprise software company, saw an 8% increase in deal velocity and 24% higher profitability. An international hotel chain immediately realized how Proof could help them shrink their marketing spend to fewer categories, reduce their sales force and yet increase revenue. And advertising agencies have realized that by proving the impact of their creative work, they can charge more.

When CMOs don't know what is working, they often spread their spending across many different categories in order to increase their chance of hitting the mark, but that is often not a successful approach and certainly not an informed one. In our experience, it's the companies who optimize their go-to-market mix that see the most dramatic impact.

Proof helps companies succeed by showing them what's working and what's not across a given period of time. This enables you to reduce the amount of money you're spending on

How to drive engagement and reach

Engagement and reach are both very important. If you don't reach your target accounts, there is no point in communicating. Driving engagement and reach consists of five parts (1-2 were covered in depth earlier in this chapter):

1. Have the right network:

The right network is a combination of the ecosystem in your industry and your top target accounts. With the wrong network, there is no point using LinkedIn.

2. Post great content:

If you post crap, you will be associated with crap. Great posts educate, challenge and entertain their target accounts and audience. LinkedIn also has a number of tips here that can help, like knowing that 80% of all video content on LinkedIn is watched with the sound off! (So don't forget to use subtitles!)

3. Design part of the content so people are more likely to engage with it:

A. Use a lot of questions. Do you agree? Do you follow? What do you think, etc.?

B. Have a call to action that encourages your audience to follow you and your team. Here is Johans Aberg's: "If you like our stuff, please follow me, Next State and my colleague XX. Visit www.nextstate.se for more interesting stuff."

C. Have reasons for people to engage with the comments. For example, if you have a white paper or other additional interesting content that you can send people, you might have them write in the comment section in order to receive it; this boosts the reach of the post.

4. Engage with the people who are liking, commenting on and sharing your posts:
When a lot of people like, comment and share, it improves the reach of your posts. How do you make this happen? First of all, post great content that interests your audience. Second, drive dialogue with them by answering questions and writing in a way that makes the person you are having the conversation with want to answer. For example, end with a question. Make sure you tag the person every time so that she or he gets notified that you have answered. Third, check who likes, comments and shares your posts and thank them in a private message.

5. Work as a team to drive reach:
There is great power when you work as a team on LinkedIn. Let's say that you are targeting one person and your team consists of five people (illustrated below as persons 1 through 5), at least one of whom has the target person as a first-hand connection.

Step 1: Person 1 posts a great post
Step 2: Persons 2-5 like and also either share or comment on the post

As a result, the post will be pushed out into their greater network. The more people who have the target as a first-hand connection, the greater the reach the post will get. Now imagine that persons 1-5 take turns posting content, liking, commenting and sharing. Our experience and research are very clear: you will dominate the feed of your target accounts and audience.

Person 1 Target
Person 2
Person 3
Person 4
Person 5

Three ways to book meetings

Although the major challenge of signing a 25 MUSD megadeal will not be booking a meeting, this still needs to happen, and LinkedIn is often a much sharper tool than cold calling or emailing today.

We advise three simple ways to book meetings using LinkedIn:

- Alternative 1: Send a PM with a direct approach to a first hand connection. (When you have bee-swarmed them a few times as a team and they have seen videos and posts following your messaging architecture, they will be more likely to answer because they see you as a trustworthy person they want to connect with.
- Alternative 2: Send a paid IM mail with a direct approach to a second hand connection.
- Alternative 3: Send a PM with an indirect approach to a first hand connection.

Alternatives 1-2 are straightforward. We have found that the third way is usually effective if you don't have a good reason to make contact.

When someone you want to make contact with engages with your content, be sure to thank them in a private message. "Thanks for the like :)" or "Thanks for the comment :)" Their response is usually something similar to, "No probs, great content deserves a like."

This often starts a conversation where you can easily take steps toward a deeper connection, and a meeting or lunch. Often on their initiative.

Having a support team

As you are reading this, you might be afraid that it sounds like a lot of work and that there is no way your team will have time for it. Just remember Johan Bjorklund's story from the beginning of this chapter - LinkedIn is a much more efficient version of Bjorklund's spreadsheet.

If you cannot build a team who can tackle this internally, find an agency that specializes in megadeal marketing that can run the entire process for you.

Metrics and measurement

Measuring progress is, of course, important. We also recommend measuring trends over time and the following metrics (they are both activity-oriented and results-oriented).

Leading indicators

A. Number of contacts from each target account
B. Number of posts per month
C. Number of views per account

Lagging indicators

D. Likes, comments, and shares average per post
E. Leads and meetings generated

However, to understand the full effect that social selling, or of any of your channels, tools and activities have on your revenue, cash flow and profit, you need to use a multivariable regression model. This is something a team of data scientists can work out for you, or you can use an automated tool for marketing mix modeling.

EXERCISES

1. Are you using LinkedIn or other social media for social selling? If not, begin by assessing the online profiles of your team and make improvements detailed above under "Get your profile ready for social selling."
2. If you have mapped the deal ecosystem as specified in Chapter 2, use that as your blueprint for social selling. Identify which social media your key stakeholders tend to use, identify first-hand contacts and follow the key steps above under "Build your network."
3. Use the messaging architecture in Chapter 6 to hone and synchronize your team's messages across multiple platforms and all your content.

KEY TAKEAWAYS

1. Your audience needs to be connected to you and your team. We mean the top 1000-10,000 people in the top accounts and in the ecosystem you are targeting.
2. Post about what is important to your target audience. Don't post a lot about your product or solution (inside-out). Don't have a "CV profile" that says, "I am a highly motivated, results-focused manager."
3. Make sure your posts have enough editorial quality (for example: no crappy selfie videos) and follow the "Challenge, Educate and Entertain" formula.
4. Work as a team. For example, bee swarming is powerful in the hands of a group of 5-7 people cooperating around the selected accounts.
5. LinkedIn Sales Navigator's advanced lead search is a world-class tool for researching your clients' buying organizations. Use it.

CHAPTER 9

ACCOUNT-BASED MARKETING

For every megadeal there is a finite group of prospects who will hear and understand the messages around your offer, find your messages more valuable than your competitor's, and be willing to pay more for what you offer. The role of account-based marketing (ABM) is to identify, target and develop relationships with those prospects. In megadeals, ABM helps you show how your offer fits with a key initiative, build consensus in the buying organization and in the surrounding ecosystem, and reduce the perceived risk around a potential deal.

As a strategy, ABM involves shifting your focus from generating lots of leads to nurturing highly targeted accounts. These accounts are specific organizations and companies that have the best possible fit with your product or service. Each account should be treated like its own market, and each one should have a strategy tailored directly to it. You can't define ABM without also defining account-based advertising (ABA) and account-based sales (ABS). Each of these is required for a fully effective account-based experience (ABX). Account-based marketing relies on ideal customer profiles and account-specific knowledge to be able to create or select content for the right channel with the right message.

In our research, we found that among B2B companies, it's almost always the case that 25% of the customer base contributes 80% of the revenue. A lot of companies would have, for example, fewer than 25 accounts representing half of their total revenue and 2,000 accounts representing the other half. But among companies who make megadeals, it's more extreme: 1-5% of their accounts represent more than 85% of their total revenue. Those numbers are rarely spoken about publicly because these companies are often publicly listed and investors might see this as a risk. (Although as we mentioned earlier, this might actually be the reason they are so successful.)

Despite this clear division of revenue, many companies are still running the same kind of marketing campaigns, and sending the same email to all of them. Most simply pay too little attention to their top accounts and too much attention to the long tail relative to the money earned.

There are two reasons for this. First, because most marketers focus on the instant feedback of lead generation, they end up spending too much time on the top of the funnel. By the time sales takes over, marketing says: "Okay, we have done our job."

The other reason is that sales does not generally understand how marketing can accelerate business at the bottom of the funnel. Matt Senatore, Service Director, Account-Based Marketing at SiriusDecisions states that their research shows an increase in deal size related to the use of ABM, but that it can still be challenging for some companies to execute. "The problem we see is that sales may say they want support, but because they really don't understand what marketing will contribute, they don't want to invest the time."

Remember, the sales funnel in megadeals is shaped like a T, not a V. When you work on big deals, lead generation is not the most expensive or time-consuming part, it's the process of driving leads from a first meeting to a deal of ten or fifty to a hundred million or a few billion dollars.

Entire books have been written on account-based marketing. Our intention with this chapter is not to fully educate readers on the topic, but to provide an approach for how to apply ABM to a megadeal.

Here are the five main reasons to use ABM when pursuing a megadeal:
1. ABM can position your company as a key part of the solution in order to succeed with one or several key initiatives.
2. It can also position your company as the given choice in the ecosystem, and the market leader/best choice when it comes to solving their key initiative.
3. ABM can help you drive consensus around the Change drivers, Why category, Why subcategory, and Why this vendor.
4. It enables you to scale up lead generation within one account. This includes finding Trojan horses.
5. It also reduces the perceived risk of your category, subcategory, and company as a vendor.

If you can integrate the approach that follows and execute it with mastery, you will experience a quantum leap, and join the ranks of those companies who already do it well. After you've read this chapter, if you think you belong to that group and are already executing our approach with mastery and at scale, please reach out to us. We would love to talk to you and exchange ideas and learnings.

ABM helps make your sales lead/team known in the ecosystem
As explained in Chapter 12, enterprise social selling is important in order to enter many parts of an organization and the rest of the deal-related ecosystem. Part of a great, well-executed ABM strategy is to accelerate social selling. This is achieved by having great content that delivers insights around Change drivers, Why category, Why subcategory, Why this vendor. It is also achieved by marketing your sales lead and building her into an expert and thought leader.

An important struggle megadealers often face is the tendency to rely too much on a few stakeholders to do the internal selling for them.

LACK OF ACCESS

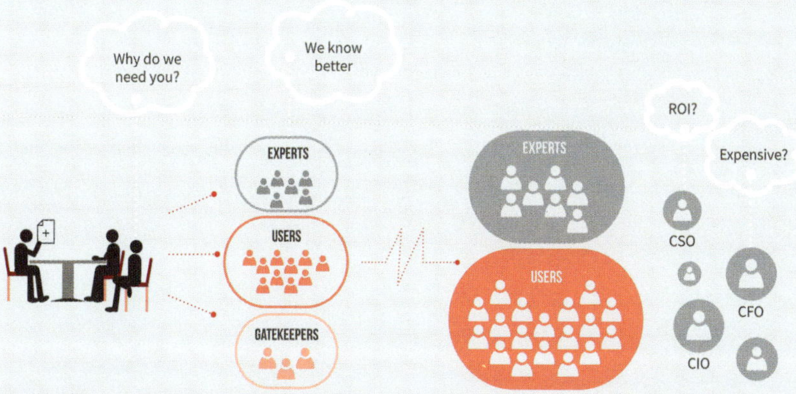

In a megadeal there are many known and unknown stakeholders who are both expensive and hard to reach.

PEOPLE ARE MORE LIKELY TO RETAIN YOUR MESSAGE IF IT IS CONSISTENT

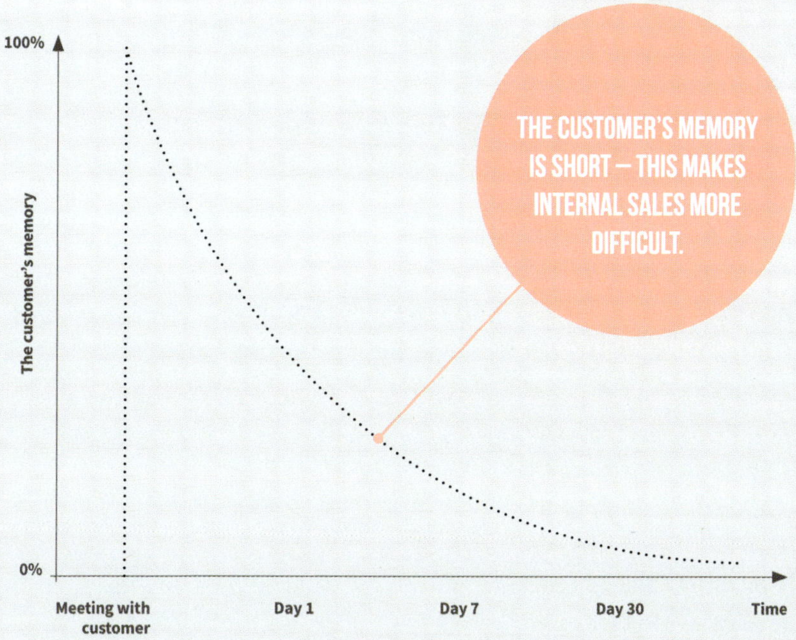

Unfortunately, those stakeholders will not remember your great pitch or the related details, but instead make up their own version. A good parallel to this is to think about how long it takes to train a new person to win megadeals for your organization. Imagine giving a new, important salesperson an onboarding of 40 hours and then asking them to sell your case inside the buying organization and the rest of the deal-related ecosystem.

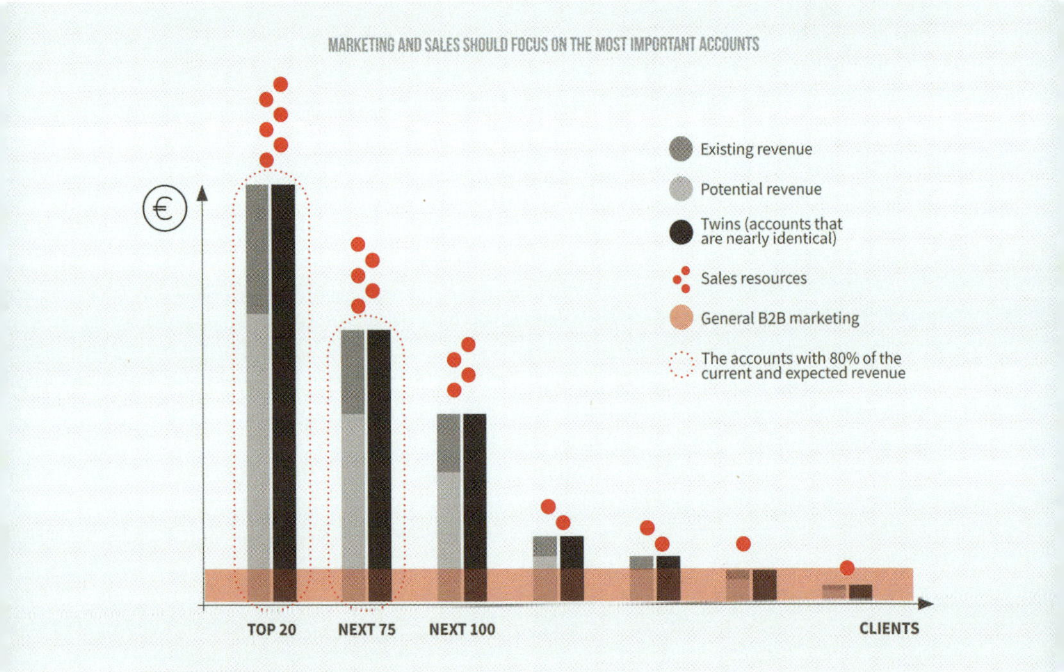

How to get started

The first step in ABM is to start with who you are marketing to. So instead of deciding to target banks, define the companies you will target:

- JPMorgan Chase & Co.
- Bank of America
- Deutsche Bank
- Banco Santander
- Mizuho Financial Group
- Barclays PLC

While it might not be big in Japan or other countries (yet), in many markets LinkedIn has made it pretty easy to find and target people with social advertising (we touched on some aspects of this in the social selling chapter). Within LinkedIn, for example, you can make an extremely targeted media buy. However, the risk is that large numbers of people are not frequenting LinkedIn. So if you are only posting once a month, you will not reach those individuals. By simultaneously targeting the same companies in Facebook and by using IP-targeted display advertising, you can increase your likelihood of reaching your target audience. This is an illustration showing the key components in an ABM marketing strategy around a megadeal.

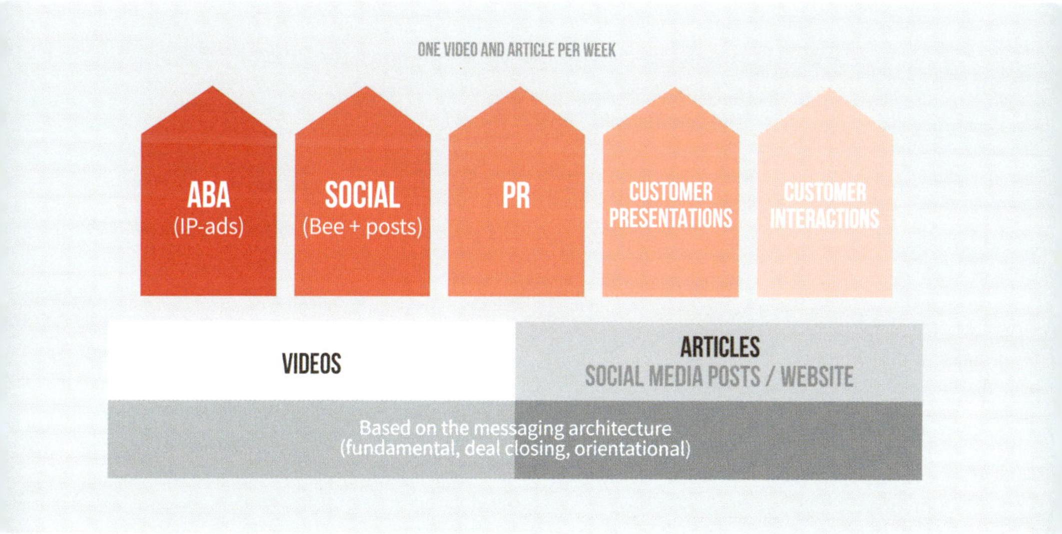

Regardless of the channels you choose, ABM enables companies to target their ideal customer profile and identify those who are willing to pay more, stay with them longer, and close faster. This is what makes ABM so effective in a megadeal: it concentrates your resources where you are most likely to win big business. While a normal marketing strategy is often applied to a range of potential clients, ABM is focused on the accounts – the key clients – that matter most to your business.

How to use intent monitoring

Another way to identify which accounts to target is by using intent monitoring. Intent monitoring (both first and third-party) helps to identify a change in buying behaviors among key prospects by looking for evidence of interest, or "intent." Intent monitoring can be used to identify patterns early, among organizations that are starting to become interested in you, to monitor your consensus-building efforts.

There are many ways to monitor intent. You can look at how many people are visiting your website and for how long, and see this as an indication of their readiness to purchase. You can also monitor IP addresses on third-party media, and/or follow searches and reading patterns. You can assess how much information they normally consume versus how much they increase their interest/consumption. You can also track the number of unique users, and see when an increase in unique users is consuming a given topic, or if the number of unique users performing searches increases.

Note, however, that intent monitoring is an advanced step. Most companies struggle just to use the right messaging and work as one team. We recommend that you master the basics of ABM first, before taking this on.

Marketing's credibility problem

Many B2B marketing teams, especially in megadeal companies, have major problems becoming credible and earning trust from management. There are many surveys on this topic, and our interviews confirmed it: Marketers have a major difficulty showing measurable results that drive revenue growth and profitability.

That lack of measurable success takes away a lot of authority and trust from marketing departments. Well-executed account-based marketing changes that. If you are a CMO or a marketer, read this chapter thoroughly.

The six key areas of account-based marketing

There are six major areas of account-based marketing to master when you're going after megadeals. This chapter is constructed around these areas.

1. Account prioritization
2. Goals for account-based marketing
3. Deciding on approaches/channels
4. Messaging architecture
5. Sales and marketing alignment
6. Measurements, follow-up and improvements

1. Account prioritization

Account prioritization is a key step in account-based marketing where you decide which accounts to focus on.

During the ABM work we have run throughout the years, we have sometimes come across questions regarding the need for deep analysis of the accounts before we engage in ABM. In almost all cases in megadeal companies, it actually (not surprisingly) turns out that management and/or the top salespeople know intuitively which companies to focus on. Either because that's where the revenue is coming from, or that's where the revenue will most likely come from in the future.

What we have found in our research is clear: Among B2B companies, it's almost always the case that 25% of the customer base contributes 80% of the revenue. In megadeal companies it's more extreme: 1-5% represents more than 85% of the total revenue. Those numbers are rarely spoken about publicly because they are often publicly listed companies and investors might see this as a risk. Although as we mentioned earlier, this might actually be the reason they are so successful.

Because of this, account prioritization can usually be quickly accomplished in a workshop format and doesn't require months of data collection.

If you research major martech companies online, you will find that many have not really understood what ABM is about. They use so many accounts in their ABM approach that it becomes impossible to move the needle inside the buying organizations.

For megadeals, it is essential to concentrate your efforts on, in most cases, fewer than 25 accounts. This will make it possible to push resources through and make a real difference. The results of our research have made it crystal clear that to win with ABM, choose fewer accounts so you can afford to expend the necessary resources.

ABM will, in many cases, require a decent amount of time and spend (in proportion to your current and/or expected revenues and profits). It is therefore important to have a realistic time frame and budget so that your campaigns actually bring about the expected results.

Smart questions to ask when prioritizing accounts:

1. Which are the most important accounts and/or sub-accounts prioritized by your company/division/country/organization for the next 12-18 months?
2. Which accounts are most likely to come under heavy attack from your competitors during the next 12-18 months?
3. What are the accounts' biggest opportunities right now?
4. If your CEO and board were to have a workshop around the most important clients to win, grow, and protect, which 15 accounts would they/you come up with? How much of your focus is on those customers?
5. If you are using intent monitoring, which accounts are showing buying signals, like activity outside their typical pattern?

2. Goals for account-based marketing

Over the years we have talked to many B2B marketers. When they are asked about the goals of their marketing efforts, many of them say things like: awareness, leads, clicks, google rankings, number of downloads of a whitepaper, open rate of emails, etc. However, most of these goals are related to lead generation. Driving business in a megadeal is less about driving lead generation and more about influencing the masses (the ecosystem) in the right direction.

Ultimately, however, you want to show that your ABM is leading to increased revenue, cash flow and profit. To do that, you need to use a regression-based marketing mix modeling - either using a team of data scientists or an automated tool like Proof Analytics. If you are not using any of these approaches, you will not be able to make sense of your metrics.

When you categorize goals, it's important to approach the endgame with milestones. Milestones are the indicators that you are on the Yellow Brick Road that leads to Oz.

Endgame/lagging goals:

- Increased win rate
- Increased deal and client size
- Shortened the sales cycles (deal velocity)
- Increased loyalty
- Lower cost of marketing and sales per earned dollar

Milestones/leading goals:

- Consensus building
- Risk mitigation (confidence and trust, etc.)
- Lead generation
- Out-position the competition

To enable the leading goals, it can be relevant to look at micro-goals such as clicks, site visits, number of white paper downloads, etc. However, these measurements need to be account-based in order to be relevant. ABM works best when applied to the bottom of the funnel, but the bottom of the funnel can be difficult to measure against number of leads.

"The #1 mistake people make is to think that ABM is a lead generation idea," says Sangram Vajre of Flip My Funnel and Co-Founder and Chief Evangelist of Terminus. "But what I've seen - after working with hundreds of companies - is that the best place to start applying an ABM strategy is at the bottom of the funnel. Even though you won't see an immediate effect on revenue, ABM helps you focus on building credibility, which will impact your pipeline and deal velocity."

It is important to know that a megadeal doesn't move linearly. It often proceeds as in the graph below. As Mark Stouse told us, "A quality ABM program will have an impact on the bottom of the funnel first but will gradually improve the size and number of deals in the pipeline."

Hence, marketing to win megadeals is often closer to lobbying than to classic marketing focused on lead generation. Because of this, it can be difficult - if not impossible - for the human brain to correlate, attribute and quantify the results, especially in long sales cycles. Using marketing mix modeling, either manual or automated, will give you insight into delayed effects like deal velocity, win rate and deal size.

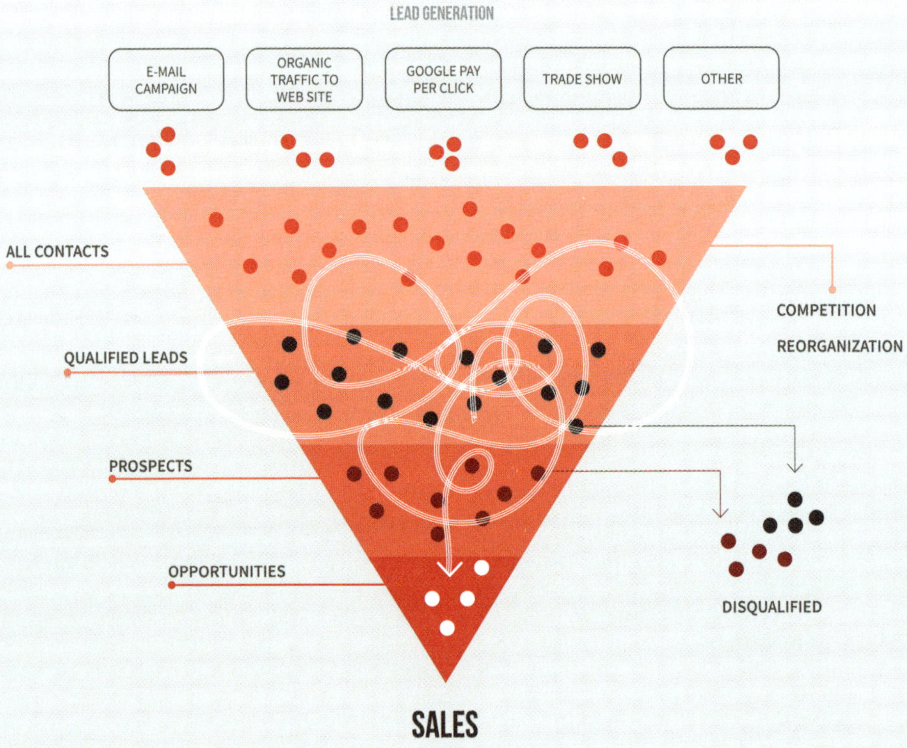

3. Deciding on approaches and channels

Depending on your budget, staffing and other resources, you ABM mix will vary greatly. It will also depend on other factors, like:

1. What goals and milestones are you trying to reach?
2. Are you targeting a few (under 10) accounts? Or many (over 30) accounts?
3. Are you targeting a few key stakeholders (under 30) or your extended target group (over 200) within one account?

Account-Based Advertising (ABA)

Account-based advertising has three major parts:

1. IP-targeted banner ads
2. IP-targeted retargeting ads
3. Social media account-targeted/sponsored posts

IP-targeted banner ads are online ads shown only to people working in the account/organization you want to influence. When an employee

ACCOUNT-BASED ADVERTISING (ABA)

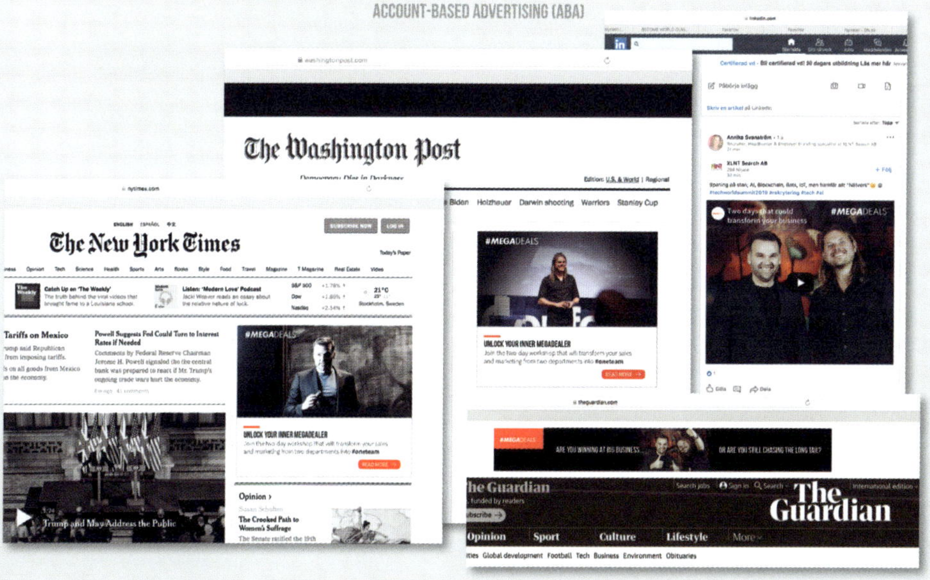

in the target organization visits an online publication (newspaper, etc.) or social media like LinkedIn, while using the company network or wifi, they will see your ads and not generic ads. The strength and weakness of IP-targeted ads is that the ads are shown to all employees within the target account. When you are pursuing a megadeal, the cost is often offset by the large number of people you need to reach and the value of the deal. For small B2B deals, IP-targeted ads are generally not recommended because of the cost ratio between the audience size and your deal value.

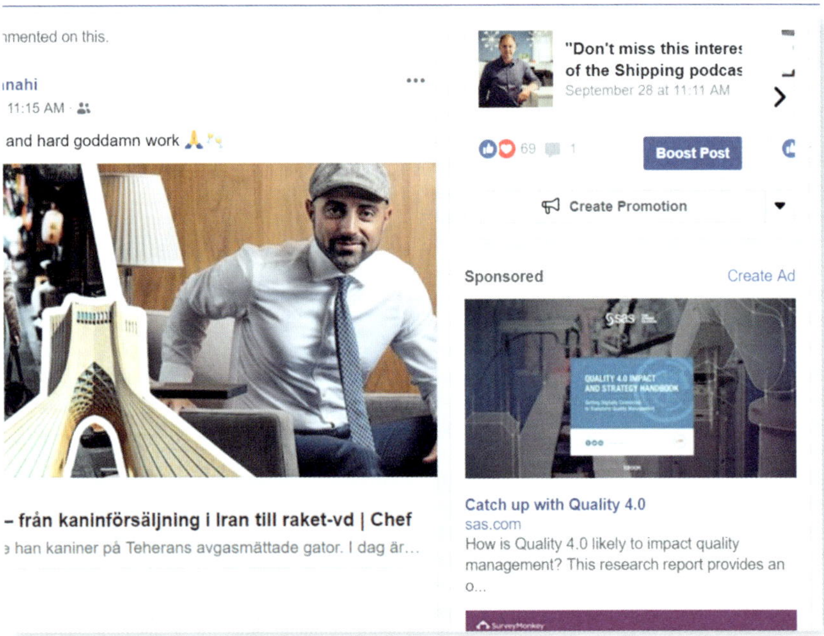

IP-targeted retargeting ads are like IP-targeted ads seen only by employees in the target account, but they are only seen by those who have also visited your (or the advertiser's) website. I.e., to see these ads, you need to be in the right organization and have visited the advertiser's website where a cookie was placed in your browser. A cookie is a text file that discloses that your computer/phone has been on a specific website.

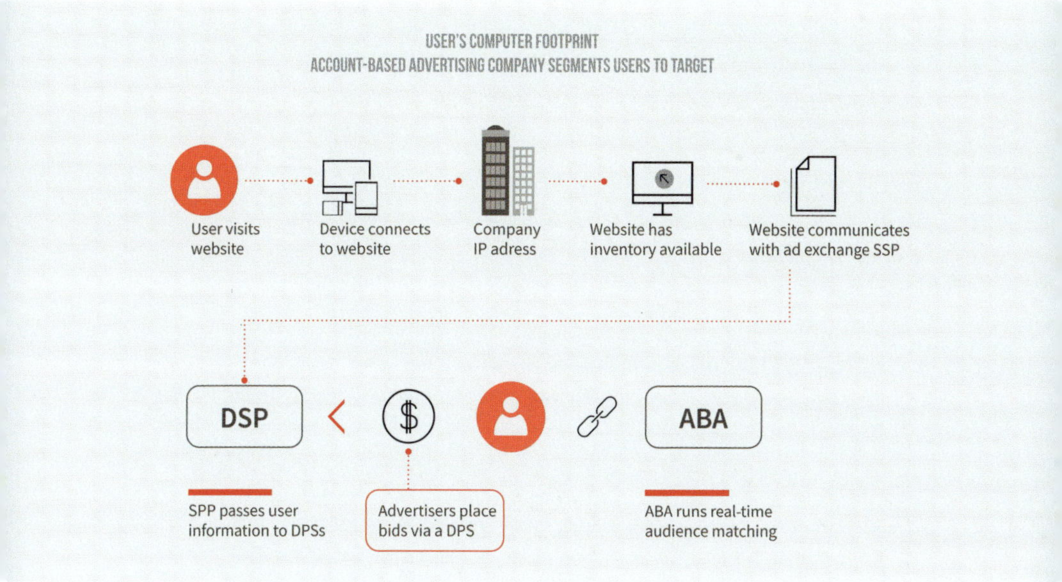

A cookie can be read by the website that gave you the cookie, but a cookie cannot by itself read your hard drive.

Nicky Briggs, Research Director of Account-Based Marketing at Sirius Decisions, pointed out that, "When many people within the buying organization are anonymous, you can use account-targeted display advertising to provide air cover to ensure that key messages are being reinforced and that you remain top of mind even if members of the buying group remain hidden throughout the buying process."

Social media account-targeted/sponsored posts

In many social media networks, you can target by employer and sometimes other parameters. LinkedIn, for example, has a vast set of targeting criteria where employer is a popular one. This can be combined with other attributes like company function, seniority level, geography, etc. With these attributes you can really zero in on the right people in the right accounts. This very precise targeting is the biggest strength of LinkedIn. The weaknesses are that not everyone is on it, and that the frequency with which each employee uses it can vary substantially.

Also, many top executives in large companies are drowning in contact requests and InMails. Account-targeted LinkedIn posts are, however, recommended in the marketing mix for ABM and megadeals.

Direct mail/email and InMail

In today's digital world, direct mail has been almost forgotten. It can be deployed in several ways. We recommend two different approaches.

1. Creative high-impact mail pieces that bring value to the people who receive them. We have seen everything from fire extinguishers to small drones being used*. Of course, there should be a strong creative connection with the client, creative piece, and communication.
2. An example sequence that has proven successful. A combination of direct mail, personal emails, and In-mail via LinkedIn:
   A. Non-corporate letter with handwritten receiver address information. The letter contains a short description about the challenges this company should have right now relevant to her/his role. At the end of the letter it also states that you will later reach out to the receiver.
   B. InMail via Linkedin with almost the same content as the letter. Just change it slightly to not have the exact same text.
   C. Email that also contains the same core messages but rewritten with different wording.

** Be aware of any local legislation like GDPR that may hinder your campaign.*

Direct mail is a great lead tool for targeting smaller groups of people. The methods above are oriented to reach fewer than 500 people in total due to the amount of manual work involved.

Make sure to measure all steps of the campaign: open and response rates, website visits, etc. To those people who respond, have a senior salesperson reach out via phone or book a meeting through LinkedIn.

Often you will get responses before you get to the final call to action. Make sure not to be over-salesy.

Our experience from hundreds of these campaigns is that there is a balance between reaching through the clutter and having the person we are approaching become upset about the campaign.

"Remember, an account does not buy - people buy," says Mark Ogne. "So you can't just deliver an impression, you have to make one. You do this by curating valued content in the buyer ecosystem, and by developing relationships."

Webinars and lunch-and-learns

Webinars and lunch-and-learns are educational presentations that you do at the client's office or over Skype for typically an hour and, in the case of lunch-and-learns, while the participants eat. It is a great tool to reach more people in the buying organizations.

Part of what is really important in the messaging architecture is that the majority of the content produced is not product marketing. (Even though, in most B2B companies, it is the other way around.) A simple rule is that people want to listen and learn about what is important to them - and that is typically not your product or solution. This is no different; so make the lunch-and-learns so educational that you theoretically could charge for them.

Outdoor advertising

Though straightforward, this is not the most common way to use ABM. That said, outdoor advertising can be very effective. In many cities, you can direct where you're buying outdoor media down to the specific placement outside your most important clients' or prospects' offices.

We recommend using it for a few important accounts for whom you want to create awareness. Then, in steps two and three, build consensus and mitigate risk when you have an important, large, extended target group that works at the head office, for example.

Marketing automation

Marketing automation and inbound marketing are traditionally used more towards SMB segments than megadeals. Using marketing automation in megadeals can be risky business and actually jeopardize entire deals. The reason for this is that, as you probably know, in many cases you have to communicate with key stakeholders high up in major organizations. They tend to respond badly to semi-automatic mass emails that are poorly tailored to them personally. If you have 30 key stakeholders, please use personal communication with them.

Nonetheless, there are two special cases where marketing automation can be a great tool when going after megadeals.

1. The transactional deals inside the ultra-complex deal.
It is unlikely that a megadeal involves only one major deal. Instead, it consists of a combination of large contracts, service agreements, smaller orders, orders for other markets, etc.

This means that an ultra-complex megadeal can also consist of transactional selling that could add up to hundreds of millions or even billions of dollars in sales. This type of selling is often done further down in the organization, and more toward decision makers, i.e., many smaller orders. Here is where we primarily recommend using marketing automation.

2. Communication to your extended target group (100+) within an account.
Within most megadeals there is an extended target group of over 100 people or more who are not directly involved in the deal but can influence it in different ways. These people are great to focus your marketing automation effort on, but keep in mind that they often are very influential people and that the quality of your marketing automation program needs to be great. Clarification: this is prioritized much later than all other ABM activities. Don't start here just because you have a marketing automation system in place.

Personalized content

A lot of very bad content is produced both by small and large companies. Getting the right content in front of the right stakeholders is at the core of account-based marketing. The messaging architecture is covered later in this chapter. In megadeals ABM, it is common to tailor content towards individual accounts.

Matt Senatore recommends creating an "overarching win theme" in large must-win deals, that addresses the motivations of the most important stakeholders. "You can then translate it down to individual components for different champions - the one in IT, the one in sales or whoever's closest to the account."

Reports, case studies and presentations are great for tailoring. For example, big consulting companies produce a lot of in-depth reports that are tailored and even branded, making it easy to adjust the graphic identity so that their clients can promote it internally without looking biased.

The personalization of websites can have different components, and martech companies keep developing new ways to personalize them. You can add customer-specific landing pages, and/or comments in a report that are specifically written with that buyer in mind. You can even add their logo, or quote their people. This is possible either by using cookies or the website visitor's IP, but it is dependent on what platform you use. Account-specific landing pages are an efficient way to achieve relevance. They can be very effective when you want to show different content to different people/accounts.

For smaller B2B deals, writing an entire article with one target account in mind will likely not be worth the time and effort. However, when the deal size is large enough, this is how a savvy marketing team with enough resources can go from good to great by taking parts of a standardized library of media assets and making them account-specific.

"The use of one-to-one marketing is by far one of the best practices out there," says Sangram Vajre. "By that I mean one ad and one message to one persona within an account that leads them to one landing page with super relevant content, and from there, retargeting with one direct mail and one campaign. It takes a lot of work, but the companies who do this, like Snowflake and Thomson Reuters, are highly successful."

Telemarketing

We want you to be very cautious with telemarketing. Many major enterprises use junior people to call executives as part of their marketing campaigns. The risks are similar to using marketing automation towards high-level executives.

In the chapter on consensus, we described what we call research calls. Research calls find out answers to questions like:

1. What are the key initiatives/strategic programs? (See the chapter about key initiatives.)
2. Who really decides what? Including which decision panels the decision would need to pass and the decision criteria in each.
3. Who else is involved in the decision?
4. Who are you competing against?

These types of calls should be made by senior people who can create rapport, and will help you acquire valuable information to base your marketing on.

Building a mix

Nicky Briggs told us that many of her clients at SiriusDecisions have been successful at using a mix of geofencing and LinkedIn alongside targeting in train stations and transport hubs near their account's offices. "We presented DXC Technology with an ROI award in 2017 for their pursuit marketing ABM strategy. From a tactical perspective they were using a mix of LinkedIn ads, social profile optimization of their sellers, account-targeted newsletters and magazines, email campaigns, web personalization, PR and commuter-targeted ads."

From account-based advertising and display ads like Vendamore's to targeted posts on LinkedIn, ABM appears in many fragrances. Regardless of which tactics you choose, creating a mix in a long-cycle B2B business needs to be focused less on MQLs and more on building awareness, confidence and trust. Most companies we know select their mix based on gut feeling. Some use a marketing mix modeling approach to select which tactics have the highest return.

Once you've got the right mix, it will drive demand and your customers will reach out to you.

Remember, no matter what mix you use, be sure to create quality marketing that adds value, helps people, challenges their beliefs and, if possible, entertains them.

4. Messaging architecture

We have dedicated an entire chapter to messaging architecture and content because of how important it is. It has been mentioned in other chapters as well.

For ABM the messaging architecture is absolutely key. Your target audience within your client accounts will have different attitudes towards your product. Many of them will be either negative or neutral to it. Just a few will be positive or actively drive the deal forward. Depending on your endgame and milestones (described under Goals for account-based marketing) the type of communication you will create will be different.

Because this detailed understanding of the client resides with the sales team, Pål Lind, CEO at InZynk, feels that messaging and content should therefore originate from sales and not from marketing. "Marketing's role is to be the responsible party for using those insights and messaging in concrete articles and videos. Marketing should also use the sales team in the account-specific content in order to raise their profile inside the target account."

Below we have listed a fundamental prioritization of communication. There is a more advanced version of this, but we have noticed that 9 out of 10 companies have extreme challenges mastering even this fundamental level. Go to Chapter 7 to get a deeper understanding.

The most important thing is that you get started - so if you already have a content model you feel is working, or it takes time to develop your messaging architecture, we recommend that you start by selecting appropriate content for your targeted accounts.

5. Sales and marketing alignment

One common problem in large multinationals is the lack of alignment between sales and marketing. This is especially true in many megadeal companies where marketing sometimes, unfortunately, can be seen as an event and/or brochure supplier - we've even heard it called "the ice cream and balloon department."

Marketers that don't understand the sales side of megadeals will not win the confidence of the global account managers or the leadership team, nor will they be able to deliver the right value to the company

TOP PRIORITY: FUNDAMENTAL MESSAGING - ONE PER AUDIENCE AND SOLUTION COMBINATION

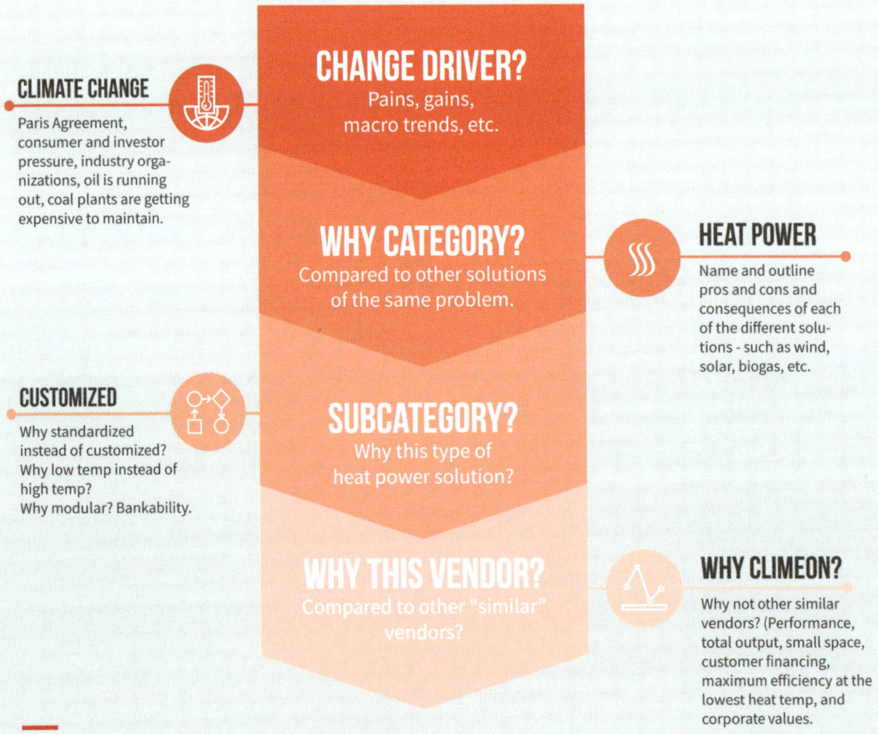

Throughout the book we use Climeon as an example because this is one of the companies that has implemented this way of working.

to fit in the role of "Megadeal Account-Based Marketer" or "Megadeal Marketer."

Reading, understanding and applying this book as a marketer is guaranteed to add credibility in the eyes of your top management and sales leadership. It will also help your company to be more successful.

Again, Sangram Vajre, "The whole last decade was about using inbound as a strategy, but today the strategy is ABM. In the next decade I foresee that marketing will be less focused on leads, and more focused on known accounts - business that sales wants to close. It will be marketing's role to inform the executive suite about the pipeline, and provide forecasts around which deals have the highest likelihood to close based on the close rate. That is the future. Where marketing can support the front end and the back end of the business outcome."

Even today, the current state and the future state of selling consist of an integrated model where sales and marketing are intertwined. In the highest functioning teams, because sales understands ABM, they are able to cooperate with marketing, and to understand how to blend sales and marketing efforts. As marketing mix modeling becomes the norm in large corporations, we will likely begin to see ABM programs evaluated based on their correlation with revenue, profit and cash flow.

ABM maturity

To apply all aspects of ABM to all important accounts in all countries is overwhelming. Instead, start with a narrow scope and create step-by-step successes.

In making megadeals, it is key that you understand the ecosystem and then drive the ecosystem towards consensus. ABM and account-based advertising are rather manageable ways to start. For example, select the top priority accounts in an industry and a country. For these you should collect the best insights (e.g.: a few articles, reference cases and videos) that you want many people in the target accounts to consume or be influenced by. You then promote these insights in banner ads and show them in an online media mix targeting those few accounts' IP numbers. This service is provided by companies like Vendemore, Demandbase, Jabmo, MRP, Terminus, InZynk, Madison Logic, etc.

Get the account-based advertising going first. Then increase the number of accounts, involve salespeople with the account-based advertising, and fine-tune it with a few iterations. Once this is in place, and is being worked on in a co-op between sales and marketing, you can gradually add the account-targeted posts on LinkedIn, and thereafter the lunch-and-learns, direct mail, and in select cases, outdoor advertising. ABM can be made infinitely complex. We could write a second version of this chapter for the few that are cutting edge. However, based on our experience and all our interviews, most companies have a lot to improve in this domain.

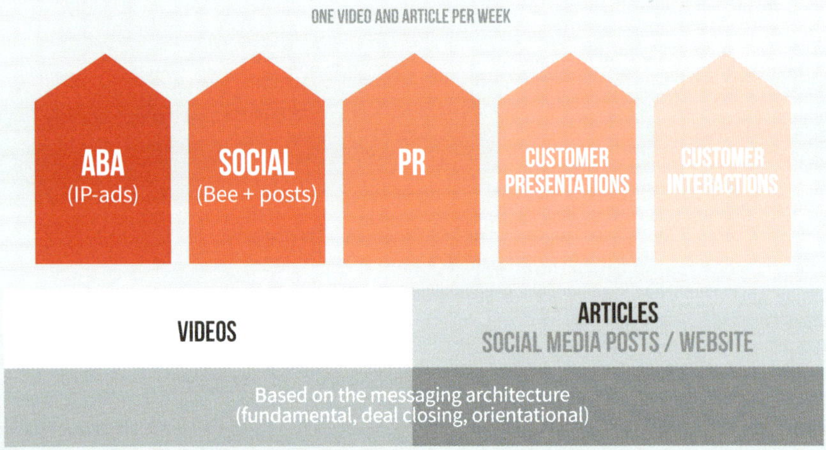

You will be on the fast path to success if you can deploy a mix of IP-targeted ads, organic social posts and paid targeted posts with great videos and articles, while running bee-swarming as a team, and making sure the greatest stories also get PR. Don't forget to base the content on the messaging architecture, placing more weight on videos. Mastery is key. If you manage to get the basic recipe for ABM going (pictured above) and execute it really well, you will find yourself ahead of the curve and reap substantial benefits. Execute this really well before you dabble in more complex forms of ABM.

6. Measurement, analytics and improvement

A fundamental problem in B2B marketing and sales today is the idea that there is a "hand off" or explicit transfer of responsibility for a lead when an MQL becomes an SQL. This encourages marketers to focus on pushing leads through a funnel, which is why so many marketing departments continue to give so much credence to lead volume. Organizing and hosting an event that generates hundreds or even thousands of leads is therefore counted as a success, even if not a single one leads to revenue.

Because this approach focuses on individual leads, it's a poor way of measuring influence across buying decisions in customer organizations. That's because MQLs do not indicate ABM success. ABM success is achieved at the bottom of the funnel, not the top. For many marketers, however, there is a strong impulse to see ABM as part of a top-of-the-funnel approach. This negates a large portion of its value, since, as we've noted before, the megadeals sales funnel is shaped like a T, not a V. Casting a wide net for leads is a waste of resources that should be focused instead on pushing a handful of deals down the T.

ABM is based around three pillars: first, growing relationships; second, building a reputation within the customer's organization and their purchasing team; and, third, generating revenue from new opportunities and securing ongoing investment from existing customers.

As to setting goals for ABM, you want to show that your ABM is leading to increased revenue, cash flow and profit. To do that, you need to use regression-based marketing mix modeling, either using a team of data scientists or an automated tool. ABM without the right analytics is as vulnerable to misdirection as any other part of marketing.

As we mentioned above, the endgame is all about:

- Increased win rate
- Increased deal and client size
- Shortened sales cycles (deal velocity)
- Increased loyalty
- Lower cost of marketing and sales per earned dollar

To reach the end game, it can be relevant to look at micro-goals (clicks, site visits, number of white paper downloads, etc.) and examine how they are trending, particularly in the context of an overall population of customers. Remember that any given individual might be representative of a trend, or they might be an outlier, so contextual understanding and macro-analysis are key to determining what's working and what's not.

These measurements need to be account-based in order to be relevant. With regression models you can see how micro-goals correlate with the leading goals, and then with the lagging goals. In this way you can find a recipe for identifying proxies leading to the financial goals.

If you don't have the regression capability, you can show value and effect by having an A-group of accounts where you run ABM, and a B-group and sometimes a C-group among which you shift tactics to see what works best.

Whatever you do, don't use MQLs as the key metric to judge the success of an ABM program.

EXERCISE & BEGINNER'S GUIDE

Review the six key areas of account-based marketing:

1. Account prioritization
2. Goals for account-based marketing
3. Deciding on approaches/channels
4. Messaging architecture
5. Sales and marketing alignment
6. Measurements, analytics, and improvements

Rate yourself, your company and your team in terms of your knowledge and mastery of these areas.

If you rate low, our suggested cut-through method is to start by taking a handful of accounts from one industry. Look at each account and quickly describe where you are and where you want to go with them. Then look among your existing videos and content to see what you can use. With just 3 to 5 content pieces per account, you can start developing ads to promote those insights that highlight the most important messages. You'll be up and running in a few weeks.

People often want to create a huge buyer's journey with academically perfect ways of marketing. But when this becomes too theoretical it gets in the way of actually accomplishing anything. "Sloppy success is better than perfect mediocrity," says Alex Mandossian. You need to get started, and "perfect is the enemy of the good."

KEY TAKEAWAYS

1. Consensus creation with a long list of known and unknown stakeholders in the account and in the rest of the deal ecosystem is key.
2. Consensus creation on a large scale within a deal-related ecosystem or simply the target account is very expensive and close to impossible to execute only by phone and in meetings.
3. Relying on the key stakeholders' internal selling skills will give you a lower win rate and a dragged-out process.
4. ABM is based on key channels like IP-targeted ads, account-targeted social media posts, direct mail/email/InMail and lunch-and-learns.

5. Start with a few accounts, a few salespeople and only account-based advertising, then scale it up to more accounts and salespeople, and then add more channels.

PART III

MEGADEAL COMPLEXITIES

PART III

MEGADEAL COMPLEXITIES

Complex deals, and in particular megadeals, are often described as having many stakeholders, a long sales cycle, and a high perceived risk. Some define deal complexity as dependent on how much time the buyer and the seller have to work together to define the deal. However, a long sales cycle is more of a consequence than a root cause. In conventional books on complex selling, complexity often centers around application complexity alone. In megadeals, however, we have identified at least seven different important complexities that do not exist in conventional complex selling.

In this section of the book we provide readers with a deep dive into two of these complexities. While political/regulatory and cultural complexities will vary depending on your location and the countries where you are doing business, and application and delivery complexity will vary according to product/offering, the complexities associated with contracting and financing a megadeal are similar regardless of location or offering.

The seven different types of complexities that we identified in our research are:

1. Political/regulatory complexity (this is country/region and industry-specific)
2. Cultural complexity (this is country/region-specific)
3. Complexity of the buying organization (covered partly in the chapters about ecosystem, consensus creation)
4. Application complexity (application-specific)
5. Financial complexity (Chapter 10)
6. Contractual complexity (Chapter 11)
7. Delivery complexity (application-specific)

The five cornerstones covered in the first five chapters can be seen as a checklist to always tick off when pursuing a megadeal. Have you...

1. Matched your offer with a key initiative?
2. Mapped the deal ecosystem?
3. Achieved consensus among the stakeholders?
4. Identified and engaged your Trojan horses?
5. Built enough trust to mitigate risk?

The seven complexities mentioned here, however, cannot simply be checked off. They are areas you need to excel at in order to be a successful megadealer. While they can be easily understood conceptually, they take a lifetime of theory, reflection, work, training, and real-life experiences to master.

1. Political/regulatory complexity

Current studies of complex systems suggest that political systems operate on a spectrum between complicated and chaotic. In other words, heaven help you should you try to enter a market with an idea of changing the regulatory framework. What you can do, however, is familiarize yourself with the permits, laws, regulations and incentives (often political) in each market you plan to sell in. You should also familiarize yourself with the complexities of subsidies, taxes and tariffs. Knowing what grants might be available in a given market could be the difference between winning and losing the deal.

In addition to national, regional and local policies, there are industry-wide regulations that you need to be aware of. In fact, you may have to change or adapt your offering or business in order to enter that market. If you come to the table without this understanding, you risk being laughed out of the room.

2. Cultural complexity

Megadeals tend to be made across national, state and regional borders. You may have to interact with royalty, be expected to eat strange foods or hold hands with your client. Companies, too, have their own internal cultures, values and codes of conduct. As Emelie Meurk Demerud, founder of the tech search firm Hedy, told us, “When I was doing business in the Middle East I was very eager to talk business. But what I learned is that you must eat lunch, smoke waterpipe, have dinner and smoke some more waterpipe. Only then can you talk business.” Complexities like these make navigating cultural differences (and sometimes languages) an extremely desirable skill set. However, it is nearly impossible to fully master.

3. Buying organization complexity

As we have mentioned earlier in the book, the buying organization is part of the deal-related ecosystem when you are dealing with the largest companies in the world. And these organizations are often entire ecosystems in and of themselves. If you were to draw an organizational matrix, they would often look more like a cube than a square. You must know how they are structured, and how decisions are made. You must learn their internal rate of return (IRR). In large public tenders, you may not be allowed to interact with the buying organization. Megadealers must have a deep understanding of their target account, and be able to move effortlessly between hierarchical levels, countries and functional areas.

4. Application complexity

Megadeals often involve the sale of advanced systems between countries, such as aircraft, weapons systems, or satellites. For a corporation, megadeals often involve combinations of software and hardware, or buildings with associated complex systems as in a hospital or data center. These are rarely stand alone systems, but involve your own offering (the technology, for example) combined with the customer's knowledge/ technology and sometimes those of a supplier.

Because understanding these systems could take a lifetime, we recommend always bringing the sales engineers with you when selling in a technical environment. You should of course have those people with you on the account team, but if the GAM/account leader doesn't know a lot about the solution and the details around the customer application area/use case, you risk losing credibility and adding time to the project.

5. Financial complexity

The financing of megadeals can involve one or more lenders, export authorities, insurers, bonds and bond-issuing agencies. They might require the formation of special purpose vehicles, as is the case in Public-Private Partnerships (PPPs). They involve trade compliance, and budget approvals/sign-offs on many levels.

We are able to provide an introduction to megadeal financing thanks to Alexander Helling's overview of the three main approaches in Chapter 10. We strongly encourage you to read this chapter. The ability to offer different types of financing to fit your customer's needs is an important risk mitigation tool. It could also be what wins you the deal.

6. Contractual complexity

What type of contract will you use? In many cases traditional transactional contracts are not the best fit, given the complex nature of megadeals. We have provided some insight into this with the help of David Frydlinger and Kate Vitasek's insights on contracting. In it, they set out a framework for a new and increasingly popular type of contract called a relational contract. Both traditional and relational contracts come with their own set of complexities. Knowing your contracting options early on and being able to offer the best type of solution could help you out-position your competitors.

7. Delivery complexity

The delivery in many megadeals is extremely complicated, with many serial and parallel tracks including, but not limited to, the client and several third parties. Often the logistics involved in delivering the solution are many times more complex than the solution and the customer's application area. Here we recommend involving the designated program manager/project leader. However, the sales leader should know enough about the delivery to handle most customer interactions. If sales does not know enough about the complexities involved in delivery and installation, it can cost you time and credibility. Especially if the contract is already in place, it could cost you more money. We recommend that your sales team participate in project management training and a few deliveries in order to fully understand what's involved.

CHAPTER 10

MEGADEAL FINANCING

Contributor: Alexander Helling

In B2B sales, customer finance is a broad term that includes everything from trade finance tools, export credits, and supply chain finance to cash management. In a megadeal, financing is one of the major complexities involved. It can be supplied by the seller or an external third party, or it can be arranged by the buyer. In order to increase the probability of closing a deal, it is important to understand all aspects of how to finance it.

By understanding the different tools companies can use to finance these deals, sellers can increase their understanding of their customers' needs and structure a deal so that it fits those needs. Financing is therefore also a tool for mitigating your client's risk, as mentioned in the risk mitigation chapter.

If you want to add a capability to your toolbox that will enable you to add value for your customers and increase sales, this chapter is for you.

Three primary financing methods

It would take an entire book to go through all the different possible structures, so we will limit our focus to three ways megadeals are most frequently financed. They are:

- Supplier's credit
- Buyer's credit
- Project finance

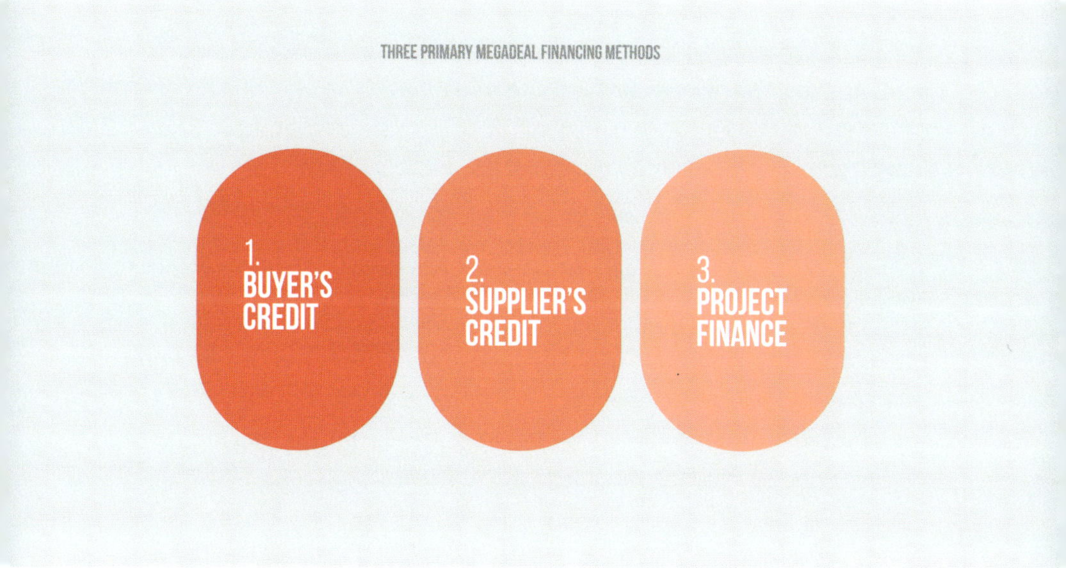

These three structures will help you understand the customer and how they might fund the purchase they are about to make from you. Many times, the buyer must get approval from various parts of the organization before he/she can sign the deal. As seen in the ecosystem chapter, this also often includes third parties. The toughest approval usually involved getting the funds from the financing department. This can be a real pain for your buyer, so if you can help them to structure the funding, it could help you win the deal. In many cases you can even save money for your customer and increase the deal value at the same time.

When you understand the above three options you will have the basic toolbox to discuss alternative financial structures with your buyer. In many cases that knowledge can support the customer in lowering their capital cost and improving their cash flow, which will enable you to demand a higher price. We would go as far as to state that adding financial structuring to your seller's toolbox will enable your salespeople to deliver higher margins and increase the speed with which they can close a deal.

To get a quick understanding of what customer finance is all about, consider the financial options when buying a car. You can buy it with cash, lease it, borrow money from your bank or get a loan from the seller's bank. What the lender pays attention to is how the security structure is set up: how the risk is managed and mitigated.

When you buy a car, you must agree to a personal guarantee. The lender quickly checks your credit rating to make sure there are no illegalities and to confirm your monthly income. However, it is not this credit check that allows you to receive favorable terms; it's the insurance structure behind the financing. Different aspects of the loan, the "facilities," are insured, bundled together and then reinsured. In other words, the lender can mitigate away all or most parts of the risk and in so doing offer you a good deal on your car.

The same concept applies to your megadeal. How can you mitigate risk in a way that gives you the best possible capital structure for you and your customer?

If set up properly, the seller can charge a higher price and at the same time lower the cost for their customer. That's how you can create a win-win situation that's profitable for both parties, and that gives you the opportunity to close the deal.

1. Supplier's credit

Have you ever wondered how governments or large companies fund their investments? How is it possible for developing countries to lend billions of dollars at long tenures at very low interest rates? How do large-scale factories, biomass plants, cement plants, steel plants or power plants fund their million or billion-dollar investments?

Let's start with the basics. By understanding the basic structure of how different financial setups can be planned, it's easier to understand the large deals made by governments and large companies, and which other players are involved.

Terms & players

1. Bank = International bank that organizes and structures the deal. The bank in this basic structure will also refinance the seller.
2. Buyer = Could be a government, government entity, private company or an SPV (Special Purpose Vehicle).
3. Special Purpose Vehicle = A new entity designed specifically for a deal or project.
4. ECA = Export credit agency (can be a guarantor, export bank, or both) .
5. Supplier's credit = Seller offers a buyer X-amount of credit time, payable at once or in separate payments over time.
6. Refinancing or discounting = a loan to bridge the cash flow gap.
7. Performance risk = The risk that the goods or services of the seller don't perform or fail to live up to the terms in the contract.
8. OECD = Organization for Economic Co-operation and Development.

How a supplier's credit is structured

In a supplier's credit structure, the seller offers X months of credit time to the buyer. Here are some reasons for a seller to do this: The credit could be a way to close the deal; the buyer might have demanded it; it might be set up to match the cash flow generated by the investment; it could also be a way to increase your profit margin by adding a financial solution or as a way to give you a competitive advantage.

If your product or service is comparable with a competitor's, and your competitor is competing with you on price, you could use the structure as an add-on service that could take the focus away from the price. A lot of companies struggle with cash flow, so if you can offer a solution that allows them to improve cash flow while at the same time making the investment possible, it could be more important for them than receiving the lowest possible price.

The supplier's credit could be backed by insurance that covers the credit risk. Insurance is vital in large deals (especially those with longer tenures) to secure a financing option that is not too expensive.

In large deals, credit risk insurance allows the seller to refinance or discount the credit for less than it would cost to borrow from their regular bank. When the credit risk is transferred to the insurance company, the bank will use the insurance company's credit rating when determining the cost of funding the refinancing scheme and in so doing be able to offer you a lower interest rate.

A supplier's credit structure is a common way for the seller to offer the customer different options to pay for the goods or services. The timespan can be everything from 30 days up to 7-10 years (or even

SET-UP

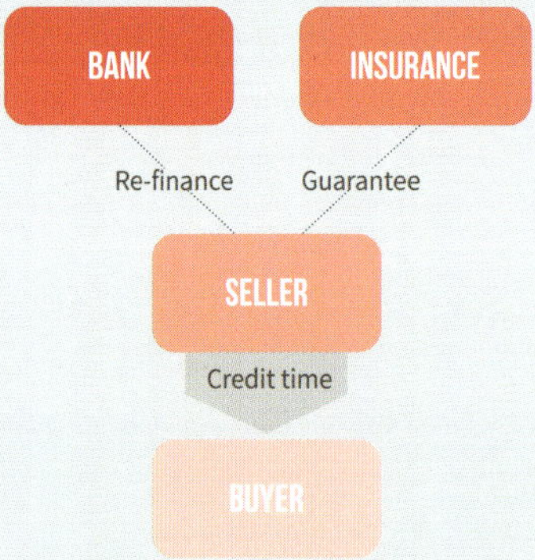

1. Seller signs a deal with buyer
2. The contract includes x-months of credit time
3. Seller insures the contract and payment obligations from the buyer with an insurance company
4. The seller re-finances the contract with its bank

PROS & CONS

BUYER

The buyers recieve x-months of credit time, resulting in:

- \+ Better cash flow
- \+ Possibility to start making money on the investment before it is paid
- \+ If the buyer has a low rating it could mean cheaper financing than alternative options
- − The credit might be expensive
- − Could take time to set up the structure
- − Could make the contract more complex

SELLER

- \+ Could be a valuable tool to close the deal
- \+ Re-financing options based on the insurance company's rating
- \+ Relatively easy to set up
- − The seller stands the performance risk
- − Could take time to set up the structure
- − Could make the contract more complex

longer) depending on the deal. If the goods are exported, the insurance and refinance is usually offered by the exporting company's export credit agency (separately or with a bank) or underwritten by an insurance broker.

Case 1: Building a heat power plant

Heat power company Climeon had a customer that was looking to invest in a geothermal heat power system. The total project budget was approximately 10 MEUR, which was too much for the customer to pay upfront. Climeon decided to engage a broker to evaluate and underwrite the credit structure and set up credit insurance. Together with the customer Climeon looked into a payment structure to match the cash flow generated by the electricity sales after installation and commissioning.

The customer paid a markup on the total price to cover the increased risk and interest that Climeon had to pay in order to secure its own cash flow. For the customer the price was higher than it would have been in a direct sales case, but the structure allowed them to speed up the installation, thus making it possible for them to start selling electricity sooner, the value of which exceeded the price increase.

This case is a splendid example of a supplier's credit structure that benefits everyone involved. Climeon was able to sign a deal and receive a better price due to the financial structure. The customer got their power plant up and running much faster, which allowed them to earn more money even though they paid a higher price.

The supplier's credit setup is quite a simple structure, but don't underestimate the time that you and your customer must spend to get all the details in place. You need to prepare financial statements, business plans, cash flow projections, guarantees, agreements, etc.

Case 2: System integration on a cruise ship

In this structure, Climeon received an order two years before delivery. Because these two years caused the company to build up costs related to material, R&D, production, QA, etc., they needed to refinance.
By insuring the sales contract with the shipyard, Climeon was able to

finance the costs taken on during those two years and at the same time make sure the company didn't get into a cash flow problem. Another positive aspect is that, once Climeon had the insurance, the company knew that if the shipyard should go bankrupt or terminate the contract, it would still get paid for all the time and costs accrued.

In this case Climeon used the supplier's credit setup but with an add-on guarantee for the manufacturing cost. Without this structure, Climeon would have had a challenging time financing the production and all the related costs.

In both of the cases above, you could use the following two ways to receive the funding and credit insurance:

Option 1

A. Use an ECA like EKN (the Swedish Export Credit Agency) to insure/guarantee the credit risk.
B. Use an export bank like SEK (the Swedish Export Credit Corporation).

Option 2

A. Use a private insurance company or a broker like BRIM or JLT to underwrite the credit risk. If the buyer has a good financial profile or rating, private insurance is more flexible than insurance from an export credit agency (ECA). They don't need to follow the Organization for Economic Co-operation and Development's (OECD) consensus rules and can structure the insurance to best fit both seller and buyer.
B. Use a local or international bank to refinance the credit.

In order to use EKN or any other export credit agency (ECA) within an OECD country, the ECA needs to follow the OECD's consensus rules. The rules state that for credit times less than 24 months, the ECA can only cover the risk in countries outside of the OECD. For credit times longer than 24 months, all countries are available, but the buyer must pay a 15% down payment and amortize at least every 6 months.

How do I know if I can use a supplier's credit as an option for my next megadeal?

When evaluating a supplier's credit setup it is important to consider the buyer's financial stability or for larger companies, their credit rating. The rating will determine the price of the insurance or guarantee, and the rating of the insurance will determine the cost of the refinance.

One important note on refinancing is the performance risk of the seller. If the refinancing bank doesn't know the seller and its products, they might be hesitant to refinance. This is a major problem for startup companies with no or few reference cases and a short credit history. (There are ways to set up the structure, which we will address later). If you are a company with a decent credit history then it shouldn't be a problem to use supplier's credit as a tool in your sales activities.

2. Buyer's credit

The supplier's credit setup is a simple and relatively quick way to offer your customer flexible credit terms, making the decision easier for the customer internally. Usually the process of getting a large investment through the internal vetting process is the most time-consuming part of large deals. If you can enable the customer to use the cash flow generated from the investment, or arrange the credit so that it matches the customer's budget, this could be what the customer needs to sign the deal.

Another way to work with customer financing is by supporting the customer in obtaining a so-called "buyer's credit." A buyer's credit is basically a loan from a local or international bank to your customer for the purchase of your products or services with a lower capital cost than the customer is able to get from a "regular" lender.

Terms & players

1. Bank = International bank that organizes and structures the deal
2. Buyer = Could be a government, government entity, private company or an SPV (Special Purpose Vehicle)
3. Special Purpose Vehicle = A new entity designed specifically for a deal or project
4. ECA = Export credit agency (could be a guarantor, export bank, or both)

5. Supplier's Credit = Seller offers a buyer X-amount of credit time, payable at once or in separate payments over time
6. Buyer's credit = The buyer receives a loan facility from a bank for the investment
7. OECD = Organization for Economic Co-operation and Development
8. Security = Credit insurance, guarantees and collateral in equipment

How a buyer's credit is structured

In a buyer's credit structure, the buyer receives a loan from a local or international bank to make the investment in your product or service. The loan is structured in such a way that your customer receives all or part of the amount needed to complete the investment.

Why can't your customer arrange financing with their regular bank? They can, but normally local banks don't have the knowledge of how to structure a deal in this way. You would usually have to get in touch with a specialized trade or export finance department at the bank to get the competence you need to set up and structure a large-scale buyer's credit.

What is different in a buyer's credit setup from a regular lender? The short answer lies in the securities of the deal. When you structure a large sales contract, the arranging bank can - if it is an export deal - insure the deal with the exporting country's export credit agency. If it's a local transaction, you could use a private insurance company to set up the structure. The insurance or guarantee allows your bank to offer your customer the loan based on the insurer's rating instead of your customer's.

In many export deals, the bank can also lend money from an ECA or export/import bank at a lower cost than if it were to use its own funds. The insurance allows your bank to mitigate the risk, which not only enables you to sign the deal, but provides much better terms.

In export deals, the arranging bank can issue a loan to the buyer even if the buyer doesn't have a strong credit rating. This is because the bank can receive a guarantee or an insurance for the loan from a government ECA. It can usually also lend money for the transaction from the ECA or export/import bank of the same country. This allows the arranging bank to set up the loan at a very low risk and in so doing also offer your customer a competitive price on that loan. Many times, at a lower interest rate than other lenders.

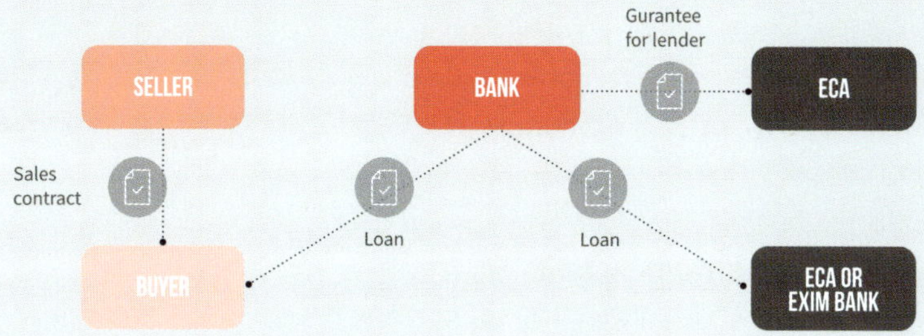

Case 1: The sale of Jas 39 Gripen to Brazil for 5 billion EURO
In 2014, the Swedish company Saab (the arms manufacturer, not the car company) announced that they had received an order from Brazil for 36 Jas 39 Gripen fighter planes at a value exceeding 5 billion EUR. This deal was structured similarly to the above example, except that the Export-Import Bank (EXIM) bank was in that case the arranging bank.

If we look at the basics in the deal that Saab negotiated, the financial setup was a key part of the contract. SEK, the Swedish EXIM Bank, arranged the credit facility to the Brazilian government at a fixed interest rate based on the CIRR system (Commercial Interest Reference Rate set by the OECD states). The loan tenure is longer than 20 years, with a fixed interest rate of 2.19% per annum. The bank could in this case offer such a long tenure and low interest rate based on the guarantee from the Swedish ECA. It's good to know that when a government is the buyer, an ECA can cover 100% of the loan - so the bank takes on no credit risk.

Example 2: The sale of Hornsea 1
Located off the coast of Yorkshire, UK, Hornsea 1 is being constructed by the Danish wind farm developer Orsted. The firm had full ownership of

the farm, but decided to sell a 50% stake in the company at a price tag of GBP 4.46 billion.

The wind farm is set to be commissioned in 2020 with an installed capacity of more than 1200 MW. The Danish ECA (EKF) covered most aspects of the deal, which included several arranging banks and tenures up to 18 years.

In cases like the above you won't have a problem finding an arranging bank. However, finding the arranging bank is usually the most time-consuming part of structuring a buyer's credit.

How do I find an arranging bank?

Arranging a buyer's credit facility takes time. If you have a large deal, above 50 MEUR, it is easier to locate the arranging bank. Make sure to first find an interested bank that can take the lead in the transaction. As mentioned above, there are usually not that many people within banks who can run, structure and get approval to take on these transactions. The larger the deal, however, the easier it is to get their attention.

If you can show the bank that the transaction you are working on will lead to more deals, this is also a way to strengthen your offer to the bank.

3. Project finance

Project finance is very similar to a buyer's credit solution. The big difference is that the buyer is usually an SPV (Special Purpose Vehicle), i.e., a new company set up only for this project. This usually means that the SPV doesn't have a balance sheet, has no assets, and no history or management in place.

So how can you fund such an SPV? With a project finance setup. A setup of this kind relies heavily on the security structure of the deal. It could be used to finance almost all types of projects and there are different structures you can use.

Usually it takes a lot of time to set up project finance, as in the buyer's credit solution, mainly due to finding an arranging bank. The bigger the deal, the easier it will be to get them onboard. It is, however, possible to obtain project financing even with smaller projects. If you would like to know more, see the case study ("Small-scale project finance") at the end of this section.

Why set up an SPV for a specific project? Why not just use your own balance sheet and fund it with debt?

The reason is usually that you don't want to have the risk on your own books. A project could be larger than your existing turnover, meaning that you couldn't fund it anyway. It could be that you are developing the project with different partners through a joint ownership SPV; there could be tax reasons or country risk reasons, etc. Usually the project owner sees an opportunity to develop a profitable project and needs funding in order to develop it.

Terms & players

1. Bank = International bank that organizes and structures the deal
2. Special Purpose Vehicle (SVP) = A new entity designed specifically for a deal or project
3. ECA = Export credit agency (could be as guarantor, export bank, or both)
4. Supplier's credit = Seller offers a buyer X amount of credit time, payable at once or in separate payments over time
5. Buyer's credit = The buyer receives a loan from a bank for the investment
6. OECD = Organization for Economic Co-operation and Development
7. Security = Credit insurance, guarantees and collateral in equipment
8. CAPEX = Capital expenditure
9. OPEX = Operating expenses
10. IRR = Internal rate of return
11. Offtake agreement = A contract to sell or buy something for a period of time

Example of an ideal case for project financing

You have an opportunity to build a project that will create a healthy return for you and your investors. However, you don't want to finance the whole project with equity and would like to add debt to the project in order to keep a larger part of the company, increase your equity IRR and decrease your risk.

Let's say that you are going to build a solar PV park and that the total CAPEX investment is 100 MEUR. The opportunity is there because you have access to a plot of land with an excellent solar index per year that would allow you to have 50% uptime. (Uptime = hours when you can produce energy that you can sell to the grid). It is also interesting because in this location energy prices are high, so you can get access to a long-term offtake agreement. You also have access to the grid so that you can connect and supply the grid with your renewable energy and a good supplier of equipment.

You basically have all the different parts in place to develop a successful project. Now you need to find the funds in order to get started.

Finding the arranging bank

As with a buyer's credit, it takes time to find and get a bank to arrange the debt facility. One fact operating in your favor is that it is a renewable energy project, because banks are encouraged internally to make more "green" deals. The size of the project is good, it's green, and you have the different parts in place to initiate the process. Usually you will meet local and international banks and their project finance departments. Hopefully you will get several banks that are fighting for the project and then you can pick and choose.

Equity injection

In a project finance setup you will (if it's not a governmental deal) need to add equity; usually around 25-40%. This equity could be supplied by you or other investors that you or an investment bank bring into the transaction

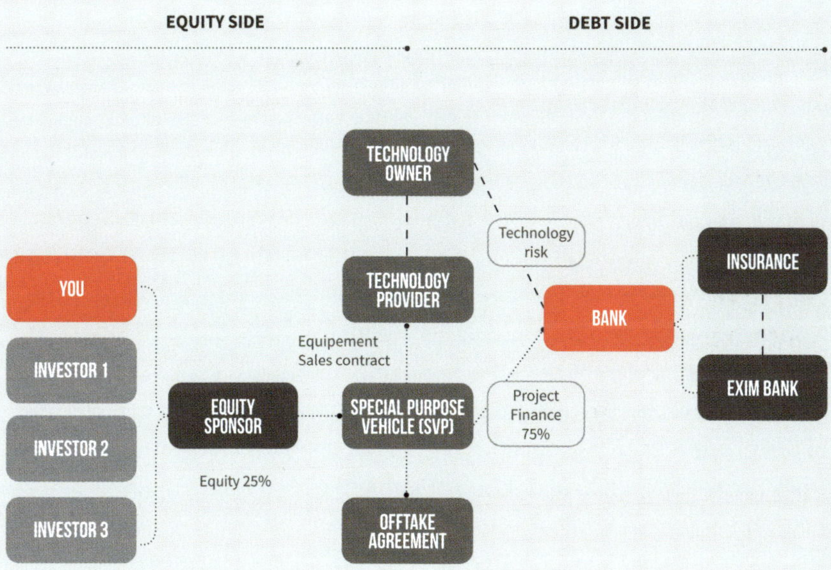

Equity side

In a project finance setup you have an equity side and a debt side. You will usually provide the equity on your own or by bringing in other investors. Normally you will build up your business case and sell it to your investors based on the structure and profitability of the opportunity.

The investors will usually demand to see a debt solution before they transfer the funds for the project. This could be a catch 22 since the arranging bank would like to see that you have the necessary equity available in order to start working on the debt solution. Normally this is solved by having the investors commit capital with certain conditions in the contract. This gives them the security that they don't need to commit all parts of the capital until the debt solution is solid.

Debt side

The debt side, or project finance facility, is where most of the work lies. First you must find your arranging bank. The arranging bank then demands all the information about the project, and as stated previously, this will usually take a lot of time to put together.

The bank will then also investigate the best security structure they can get for the project. This is typically done through an export credit agency or private insurance. They will pay a lot of attention to the technology risk. If it's a new technology, that could be a deal breaker for the bank. If the technology hasn't been around for a long period of time, the bank usually demands a guarantee from the technology provider. If the technology provider can't supply such a guarantee you might lose your bank funding.

It is important that you pay attention to the technology you will use in the project. Even if the technology is not the best on the market, the track record of an inferior technology might get you the funding while a new and better technology won't.

Example of information for a project finance case

1. Third-party perspective on technology
2. Business plan for the exporter (inc. cash flow analysis)
3. Business plan for the project (including cash flow analysis and action plan, for example if delays should occur)
4. Information about SPV (long-term business plan) and its owners
5. Description of the financial structure for the project (e.g. PPA, amortization structure, sensitivity analysis, capital structure, equity/debt ratio)
6. Third-party technology option of project design
7. Description of the risk reducing structure (e.g. covenants and security structure)

8. Description of PPA (e.g. the customer (rating, company description), tenure, and price)
9. Description of CSR (e.g. human rights, anticorruption, environment and tax aversion)
10. Agreements (e.g. land lease, building permit, energy production permit, environmental permit, etc.)
11. Company structure (SPV and subsidiaries)
12. Description of the market

The bank will also investigate the offtake agreement. When you are arranging the project, the stronger and more secure the future cash flow, the easier it will be to get the debt side approved. In energy projects, offtake agreements usually span between 10-20 years at fixed prices. The offtakers (electricity buyers) are also usually strongly rated companies. This lowers the risk that they will default and strengthens your case.

Case study: Small-scale project finance for heat power plants in Iceland
About a year ago, an Icelandic company reached out to Climeon and Baseload Capital expressing an interest in building small-scale heat power plants with Climeon's technology.

The technology is a perfect fit for Iceland, which has low temperature (70-120 degrees Celsius) water all over the island. At the time, ISOR, the local energy authority, had just published a report in which they had identified existing water wells with the potential to deliver 45 MW of electricity. Climeon could provide the technology, but needed to make it bankable. How could Climeon structure the financial setup so that it made economic sense?

Below we explain the structure and the different players that worked together to set up and make the Iceland project successful, both from an environmental a financial perspective.

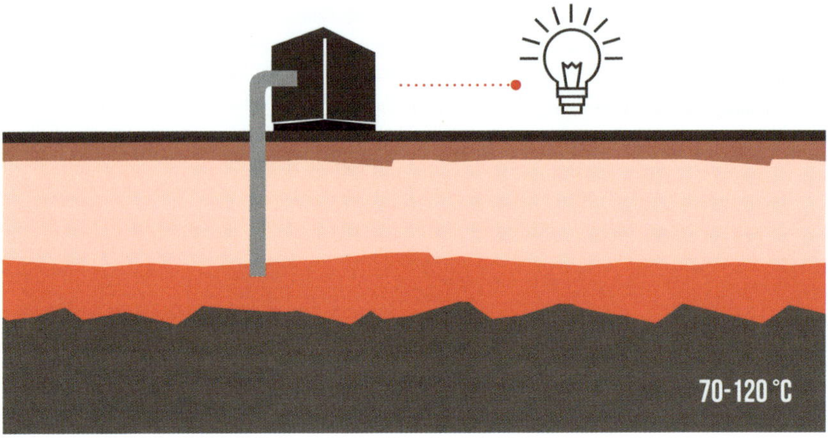

Terms & players

13. Heat power operator = the local company (usually an SPV, special purpose vehicle) that is established to run the power plant
14. PPA, offtake agreement or feed-in tariff (FIT) = the contract between the electricity buyer and the heat power operator
15. Bank = International bank that organizes and structures the deal
16. ECA = Export credit agency (could be a guarantor, export bank or both)
17. Export Credit Bank = a government bank providing funds for exports
18. Performance risk = in this case the technical risk that the resource (water supply) or equipment wouldn't work according to specifications
19. NPV = Net present value: a way to calculate what future cash flows are worth today
20. IRR = Internal rate of return: a way to calculate the profitability of the project

Iceland's energy prices are among the lowest in the world. When you build a power plant you expect it to last for a long time and generate a stable cash flow. In Iceland you can take the hot water from the ground and produce electricity that you can sell to one of the electricity companies that distribute electricity to consumers. The resource is secured by using existing wells or documented resources where it is known that there is a stable temperature and water flow. The PPA is usually set up for a 12 or 18-year tenure with a price adjustment every year.

When you know how much the resource produces and how much you will get paid for the electricity, it's easy to calculate the profitability of the project.

The long-term PPA that is available in Iceland today is about 40 EUR/MWh. With these low electricity prices, it is possible to receive a project IRR between 7-10%, which is acceptable but not enough to get early investors to jump on the project. For that you need to reach an IRR above 10%. So how do you get the IRR up? You must add leverage. I.e., it's not enough to build the power plant with your own equity, you must also add a debt side to the project. In other words, if you can borrow money you can invest less of your own money and in so doing get a higher IRR on the equity, making the project more attractive.

Example

If you invest 100 USD in a project that will generate 20 USD/year for 10 years, with no residual value and a discounting rate of 5%, you will get an equity IRR of 15%.

If you instead borrow 50 USD at an interest rate of 4% and only inject 50 USD of your own equity, you will get an equity IRR of 38%, making it much more interesting for the equity provider.

How can you add a debt side to your project?

When you want to add leverage to a project you will be directed to the project finance departments within the banks. Usually the international banks are not keen on structuring projects below 50 MEUR. This is a problem if you, like Climeon, would like to build small-scale heat power plants with investments ranging from 2 MEUR up to 30 MEUR.

First of all, you need a local bank that can arrange the deal. This bank will lend the SPV the money – but only if you can supply the bank with good enough guarantees. One way of getting this kind of guarantee is from an export credit agency, in this case EKN. ECAs can cover project risk according to the OECD's consensus rules. In this case, they could cover 75% of the bank's risk. The arranging bank then needs to have access to "cheap" capital. This they can supply themselves or borrow from an export credit bank. In this case, SEK.

So far so good, but in order to get the arranging bank interested, you need to be able to show them that you have an attractive case where they can make some money. Climeon did this by showing that building its heat power plants is very much a plug-and-play solution and that they will not build one power plant but several.

By structuring the deal in this way, you are able to show the arranging bank that it will not only be a 2 MEUR project but probably a 100 MEUR project. This creates a win-win for all parties.

The overall structure

By structuring a deal in this way you can get the bank interested in going the extra mile that is needed in order to set up a project finance solution. Additionally, by building a long-term strategy with the bank, you will speed up the process in your future projects.

EXERCISE

You are the sales manager of a company producing cutting machines for steel plates. When the steel is produced it gets delivered to your customers in large plates that must be cut into certain sizes and then shipped off to other users. For your customers the most important parts of operations are time, the speed they can cut the plates in, and energy efficiency. The biggest OPEX cost your customer has is electricity.

Your equipment cuts steel plates 10% faster than your competitors' and it also uses up to 20% less electricity in doing so. Your customer is eager to try your equipment but can't pay for the machines up front. It's a big investment, and since the steel-cutting business is a low-margin business, they must be careful about how they spend their cash and use the credit lines they have at hand.

Basic info

Price of the machine to customer: 1 MUSD
Seller's margin on a direct sale: 30%
Annual electricity savings: 50,000 USD
Extra income from 10% increase in capacity: 150,000 USD
Customer's internal interest rate: 9%
Seller's internal interest rate 7.5%

Question A:

How would you structure a supplier's credit in a way that makes both you and the customer benefit from the deal?

Question B:

How would you set up a buyer's credit for your customer, and what impact would such a solution have on your customer's available credit line?

KEY TAKEAWAYS

Knowing how to finance a megadeal can be the difference between success and failure. It is also a key ingredient in mitigating your customer's risk. There are three primary methods for financing a megadeal. They are:

Supplier's credit:

1. In a supplier's credit you offer the customer credit for their purchase and you can structure it in ways that are beneficial to both you and your customer.
2. When you arrange a supplier's credit it is important that you keep track of your own cash flow so that you don't end up with internal cash issues.
3. A supplier's credit is usually the fastest way to add funding to the deal and a tool to close the contract faster.

Buyer's credit:

1. A buyer's credit is a bank facility (loan) to your customer from a local or international bank.
2. The security structure of the deal will determine the cost of the funds.
3. Don't underestimate the time it takes to find an arranging bank.

Project finance:

1. The success of setting up a project finance solution depends on the project's risk profile.
2. Manage the risk for all stakeholders and support them with the information necessary to get them onboard. Don't rely on the stakeholders to do the job.
3. Don't underestimate the time it will take to set up a project finance solution.

LIST OF FINANCIAL TERMS AND ABBREVIATIONS

When it comes to abbreviations, it's good to know that they vary significantly between the different organizations working within the finance industry. Insurance companies don't use the same abbreviations as banks, etc. It is always good before a meeting with someone from the finance industry to go through the different abbreviations they might use so that you can speak the same language. This will help you build credibility and speed up the process.

We usually use the following sites:

Investopedia

Wikipedia

The list below is from Wikipedia:

A

AP	Accounts payable
ASP	Average selling price
agt.	Agent
a/c.	Account

B

B2B	Business-to-business
B2C	Business to Consumer
B2G	Business-to-government
BEP	Break Even Point
BLS	Balance Sheet[3]

C

CAO	Chief Administrative Officer
CAGR	Compound annual growth rate
CAPEX	Capital Expenditure
CAPM	Capital asset pricing model
CDO	Collateralized debt obligation
CDS	Credit default swap
CEO	Chief executive officer
CFA	Chartered Financial Analyst
CFC	Consumption of fixed capital

CFCT	Cash Flow Cycle Time
CFO	Chief Financial Officer
CFS	Consolidated Financial Statement
CIA	Certified Internal Auditor
CIF	Cost Insurance With Freight
CIMA	Chartered Institute of Management Accountants
CIO	Chief Information Officer or Chief Investment Officer
CISA	Certified Information Systems Auditor
CIP	Carriage and Insurance Paid
CMA	Certified Management Accountant
CMO	Chief Marketing Officer
COB	Close of Business
COGS	Cost of Goods Sold
COO	Chief Operating Officer
CPA	Certified Public Accountant
CPQ	Configure, Price, Quote
CPI	Consumer Price Index
CPU	Central Processing Unit
CSI	Continual Service Improvement
CSO	Chief Security Officer
CSR	Corporate social responsibility
CRM	Customer Relationship Management
CVP	Cost Volume Profit
C2B	Consumer-to-business
CTO	Chief Technology Officer
C&F	Cost With Freight
CX	Customer Experience
CKM	Customer Knowledge Management
CTC	Cost to company

D

DDA	Depletion Depreciation Amortization
DI	Dispatch information
DMA	Direct market access
DR	Depositary receipt
DSP	Delivery service provider
DTP	Do this please
DVP	Delivery versus payment
DSO	Days Sales Outstanding
DPO	Days Payable Outstanding

E

ECS	Electronic Clearing Service
ECS	Electronic Clearing System
EAR	Effective annual rate
EAY	Effective Annual Yield

EBITA	Earnings before interest and taxes and amortization
EBITDA	Earnings before Interest, Taxes, Depreciation, and Amortization
ECB	European Central Bank
EDI	Electronic Data Interchange
EFSM	European Financial Stabilisation Mechanism
EFTPOS	Electronic Funds Transfer at Point of Sale
EPS	Earnings per share
EXP	Export
EOB	End Of the Business
EOD	End Of the Day
EOM	End Of Message
ERP	Enterprise Resource Planning
ETA	Estimated Time of Arrival
ETD	Estimated Time of Delivery
EMI	Equated Monthly Installment
EPC	Export Promotion Council
ECGC	Export Credit Guarantee Corporation of India
EXW	Ex Works, Ready at Warehouse

F

FAB	Feature Advantage Benefits
FDP	Finance Department
FOB	Freight On Board
FIFO	First In, First Out
FinMin	Finance Minister
Fin Min	Finance Minister
FL	Financial leverage
FOMC	Federal Open Market Committee
FP&A	Financial Planning & Analysis
FPO	Follow on public offer
FIX	Financial Information Exchange
FSA	Financial Services Authority
FX	Foreign exchange market
FYI	For Your Information
FOC	Free Of Cost
FYA	For Your Action
FTE	Full Time Equivalent
F/U	Follow-Up

G

GAAP	Generally Accepted Accounting Principles
GAAS	Generally Accepted Audit Standards
GDP	Gross Domestic Product
GDR	Global depository receipt

GFCF	Gross fixed capital formation
GL	General Ledger
GMV	Gross Merchandise Volume
GP	Gross Profit
GPO	Group purchasing organization
GRN	Goods Receipt Note
GRNI	Goods Receipt Not Invoiced
GSV	Gross Sales Value
GVC	Global Value Chain
GMROII	Gross Margin Return on Inventory Investment
G&A	General and Administration expense. expenditures related to the day-to-day operations of a business

H

HR	Human Resources
HQ	Headquarters
HRD	Human Resource Development
HMRC	Her Majesty's Revenue and Customs

I

IAS	International Accounting Standards
ICB	Industry Classification Benchmark
ICRM	Innovative Customer Relationship Management
IE	Interest expense
IFRS	International Financial Reporting Standard
ILCLP	IdentLogic Systems Customer Loyalty Program
IMF	International Monetary Fund
IMP	Import
Inc.	Incorporated
IoT	Internet of Things
IPO	Initial Public Offering
IR	Interest Rate - typically referring to an IR derivative product
IRS	Internal Revenue Service
ISIN	International Securities Identification Number
ISM	Institute of Supply Management
IYR	In Year Revenue
IPT	Item Per Transaction

J

J	Journal
JIT	Just in time
JIS	Just in sequence
JST	Joint Supervisory Team

K

K	Is used as an abbreviation for 1,000. For example, $225K would be understood to mean $225,000, and $3.6K would be understood to mean $3,600. Multiple K's are not commonly used to represent larger numbers. In other words, it would look odd to use $1.2KK to represent $1,200,000.
KPI	"Key Performance Indicators" refers to a type of performance measurement. An organization may use KPIs to evaluate its success, or to evaluate the success of a particular activity in which it is engaged.
KYC	"Know Your Customer" refers to due diligence activities that financial institutions and other regulated companies must perform to ascertain relevant information.

L

LBO	Leveraged Buyout
LC	Letter of credit
LIBOR	London Interbank Offered Rate
LE	Latest Estimate
LIFFE	London International Financial Futures and Options Exchange
LIFO	Last In, First Out
LLC	Limited Liability Company
LME	London Metal Exchange
Ltd.	Limited Company
LTV	Loan to Value
LoU	Letters of Undertaking

M

MBS	mortgage-backed security
mfg.	Manufacturing
MGMT	Management
MIC	Market Identifier Code

MoM	Month on Month / Month over Month
MOQ	Minimum Order Quantity
MOU	Memorandum of understanding
MPC	marginal propensity to consume
MRO	Maintenance, Repair, and Operations
MRP	Maximum Retail Price
MSOD	Monthly Statement of Select Operational Data
MSRP	Manufacturer's Suggested Retail Price
MT	Month-to-date
MWC	Managerial Working Capital

N

NAV	Net asset value
NCBO	No Change of Beneficial Ownership
NCND	Non-Circumvent and Non-Disclosure
NDA	Non-Disclosure Agreement
NII	Net Interest Income
NIM	Net Interest Margin
NOA	Net Operating Assets
NOI	Net Operating Income
NOPAT	Net Operating Profit After Tax
NPL	Non-performing loan
NPV	Net Present Value
NTE	Not To Exceed
NYMEX	New York Mercantile Exchange
NYSE	New York Stock Exchange

O

OC	Opportunity Cost
OCF	Operating cash flow
OECD	Organisation for Economic Co-operation and Development
OEM	Original Equipment Manufacturer
OIBDA	Operating Income Before Depreciation And Amortization
OPEX	Operational Expenditures
OTC	Over-the-counter (finance)
OOO	Out of Office

P

PA	Purchasing agent
PA	Promotional Activity
PAT	Profit After Tax
PBT	Profit Before Tax
P/E	Price-to-earnings ratio
PEG	Price-to-earnings growth ratio
P&L	Profit and Loss

PI	Professional Indemnity (insurance coverage)
pip	Percentage in point
PMAC	Period Moving Average Cost
PO	Profit Objective or Purchase Order
POS	Point of sale
PP&E	Property, plant, and equipment
PPP	Public-private partnership
PPP	Purchasing power parity
PR	Purchase Requisition
PHEK	Planherstellungskosten (Product Planning cost)
PTD	Project to Date
PPt	Power point presentation

Q

QC	Quality control or Quality costs
QoQ	Quarter on quarter
q/q	Quarter on quarter
QTD	Quarter-to-date

R

RBI	Reserve Bank of India
RBA	Reserve Bank of Australia
RE	Retained Earnings
RFI	Request for information
RFP	Request for Proposal
RFQ	Request for Quotation
RFX	Generic name for a Request for Information, Proposal or Quotation
ROA	Return on assets
ROCE	Return On Capital Employed
ROE	Return on Equity
ROI	Return on Investment
ROIC	Return on Invested Capital
RONA	Return on net assets
ROS	Return on Sales
RR	Resource rent
RSP	Retail selling price
R&D	Research and Development
RC	Retail Company

S

St	Sales, during time period t.
S&M	Sales & Marketing
S&OP	Sales and operations planning
SAAS	Software-as-a-Service
SCM	Supply Chain Management
SCBA	Social Cost Benefit Analysis
SEBI	Securities and Exchange Board of India

SEC	Securities and Exchange Commission
SG&A	Sales, General, and Administrative expenses
SIR	Stores Issuance Requisition
SIOP	Sales Inventory and Operations Plan
SIV	Structured investment vehicle
SKU	Stock keeping unit
SME	Small and Medium Enterprises
SOHO	Small Office/ Home Office
SOX	Sarbanes-Oxley
SROI	Social return on investment
SOP	Standard Operating Procedure
SOW	Statement Of Work
SLA*	Service Level Agreement
SUA	Start Up Agreement

T

TCO	Total Cost of Ownership
TCV	Total Contract Value
TSR	Total Shareholder Return
TB	Transaction Banking
TBD	To Be Defined
TBC	To Be Completed
TQM	Total Quality Management
TOTW	Time Off for Time Worked
TTM	Trailing Twelve Months

U

USP	Unique Selling Proposition

V

VAD	Value-Added Distributor
VAT	Value-Added Tax
VAR	Value-Added Reseller
VC	Venture Capital
VaR	Value at Risk

W

WACC	Weighted average cost of capital
WC	Working capital
WFH	Work From Home
wk	week
wrk	work
wo	work order
WIGs	Wildly Important Goals
wasp	weighted average selling price
WLL	With Limited Liability
w.r.t	With Respect To
WTI	West Texas Intermediate
WVN	Withdraw Voucher Note
WHT	Withholding Tax

WTO	World Trade Organization
WTD	Week-To-Date
WW	World Wide

X

Y

YTD	Year-to-date
YTG	Year-to-go
YOY	Year-over-year
YTC	Yet-To-Confirm
FYF	Full Year Forecast
1H	1st Half

Z

zcyc	Zero Coupon Yield Curve
ZOPA	Zone of Possible AgreementFinancial terms & abbrivations

CHAPTER 11

CONTRACTING

Contributors: David Frydlinger and Kate Vitasek

Advanced megadealers will want to contribute to a better contracting process and better contracts, and must therefore know some basics of contracting. We suggest starting with the question: Why are contracts entered into? This may seem like an abstract philosophical question. But without having an idea of why a contract is entered into, it is hard to find alternative and better ways to design one.

What is a contract?
According to Wikipedia, a contract is a promise or set of promises that are legally enforceable which, if violated, allow the injured party access to legal remedies. This is the classical view of a contract, where the key element is *enforceability*. If the contract is breached, you can go to court and get remedies from the other party. The contract's enforceability holds part of the answer to why contracts are needed. It goes back to

the sad fact that we human beings are all opportunistic. This means we are often inclined to do what is best for us and disregard the interests of others.

Two companies in a megadeal may agree on a set of services and a price. But what if the seller wants to maximize profit by providing services of low quality, using unskilled staff and old computers? Without an enforceable contract specifying quality standards, the seller may very well do that when the time comes for the services to be provided. And what if the buyer regrets the choice of buying the services, and wants to spend the money on something else? Without an enforceable contract specifying the price and payment terms, the buyer may very well choose not to pay.

"THE CONTRACT IS, FROM THIS PERSPECTIVE, A RISK MITIGATION INSTRUMENT."

A first reason contracts are entered into is therefore this: to protect against the other party's opportunistic choices. An economist would say that the contract is entered into to safeguard the investments in time, work, money, etc. The contract is, from this perspective, a risk mitigation instrument.

But this is not the only "why" of contracts. In recent years, it has become clear that contracts also fulfill another key function and that is to prevent the parties from becoming disappointed with one another and punishing one another in different ways based on that disappointment.

Let's say a company buys a service from another company but they don't enter into a contract and therefore fail to clarify what they expect from one another. The buyer will have expectations as to which service is bought, when it should be delivered, the quality and not least the price. The seller will have similar expectations. Since all humans operate under a self-serving bias, i.e., interpret things in ways that benefit themselves, they will have contradictory expectations. The buyer will expect a high-quality service with a price close to the seller's cost for delivering it. The seller will expect a price closer to the actual value of the service for the buyer, which may exceed the cost of delivering the services by quite a bit.

> **"WITHOUT A CONTRACT SPECIFYING THE PARTIES' EXPECTATIONS, THEY WILL INEVITABLY BECOME DISAPPOINTED WITH ONE ANOTHER."**

Without a contract specifying the parties' expectations, they will inevitably become disappointed with one another. It is easy to picture the scenario playing out. The buyer thinks that the service has been delivered too late and with too low quality. Based on this, the buyer will only want to pay a very low price. The seller will be surprised by this reaction, thinking it delivered on time and with great quality. And will want a high price. Friction will arise in the relationship and the parties will start to punish one another in different ways. The seller, angry with the buyer's disappointment, may deliver even later next time and may bring in unskilled staff to the ungrateful buyer. The buyer might delay payment of the service and spread bad rumors about the seller in the market. And on it goes.

The second main reason contracts are entered into is therefore to avoid, to the extent possible, the parties becoming disappointed with one another. To avoid feelings that things are not as good as they could be in the deal because of the seller failing to meet the buyer's expectations and vice versa. And to avoid all the negative reactions, which often are expressed in opportunistic behavior, that typically follow such feelings of disappointment. The contract is therefore not only an instrument of risk mitigation but also an *expectations management instrument*.

When you approach different types of contracts for your megadeal, keep these two "why's" in mind: protection against opportunistic behavior and alignment of expectations. For, depending on the deal, these functions can be fulfilled more or less easily by different contract forms.

The contracting challenge

Many dealmakers see the contracting process as a painful tearing apart of a great deal. The excitement wanes when the lawyers enter; contract negotiations are taken to a new level with constant reiterations, red-lines going back-and-forth in seemingly endless negotiations over details and risks that may never come to fruition. Previously trustful and open discussions become distrustful and guarded. Formerly rational business people turn risk averse as soon they hear the word "contract" – especially if their legal counsel insists on standardized risk-shifting clauses that are touted as "corporate standard practice."

Finally, after the lawyers are done, the ink is dry on the signing pages, and the champagne bottles are empty - the contract goes in a drawer and is only consulted if there is a serious disagreement. Often key stakeholders responsible for delivering on the contract have never even read it. Why all the painful negotiations for a set of documents that no one cares about?!

Paradoxically, contracting professionals agree that the typical contracting process is less than optimal. Let's look at the biannual "Top Terms" report from the International Association for Commercial and Contract Management (IACCM). The ten most frequently negotiated terms in 2018 were:

1. Limitation of liability
2. Indemnification
3. Price/charge/price changes
4. Termination
5. Scope and goals/specifications
6. Warranty
7. Performance/guarantees/undertakings
8. Payment
9. Data protection/security/cyber security
10. Liquidated damages

For anyone who has experienced the risk-averse negotiations of many megadeals, it should come as no surprise that limitation of liability and indemnification top the list. What is surprising is that when the same respondents are asked, "If the aim of contract negotiation is to create a framework for successful business outcomes, do you believe that negotiations today focus on the right topics to achieve that aim?" almost 75% say no! When asked what they believe are the most important terms to negotiate, the picture changes. In the 2018 report, scope and goals/specifications and responsibilities of the parties top the list; limitation of liability fell to number seven and indemnification did not even make it into the top 10!

Clearly, something strange is going on if the people who draw up the contracts year after year report they aren't negotiating the most important terms.

What are the reasons behind these somewhat contradictory and depressing results? "Resistance from the other side" is the most common reply. In other words, everyone is blaming everyone else.

With business people blaming lawyers, and lawyers blaming each other, the better question is: How can we spend less time on a pointless blame game and more time ensuring the deal will be successful?

> **"THIS POSES A REAL PROBLEM IN MEGADEALS, WHERE THE STAKES ARE HIGH AND THE CONTRACT IS CRITICAL TO MITIGATE RISKS."**

This poses a real problem in megadeals, where the stakes are high and the contract is critical to mitigate risks. But there are also opportunities here for megadealers willing to face the challenge. A growing number of progressive contracting professionals and academics have explored alternative, more efficient and value-creating contracting methods and forms. IACCM has, for example, initiated a project to identify what they call contracting principles, by which they mean pre-written contract clauses aimed at establishing fairness from the start. And the University of Tennessee has done pioneering work in the area of using a highly collaborative win-win methodology for which researchers have coined the term "Vested outsourcing" - or simply Vested for short. Both get to the heart of a growing trend towards adopting relational contracts. In this chapter we describe the main differences between these contract forms and offer guidance on which one to choose for your megadeal.

Transactional vs. relational contracts

As a megadealer, you play a key role in determining what type of contract is best suited for your deal. There are two basic forms of contracts: transactional contracts and relational contracts. Both types fulfil two main functions: they protect against opportunism and manage expectations. Both are written, enforceable contracts; however, they are not equally well suited for all deals.

Perhaps you will recall the very public debacle in 2014 when GT Advanced Technologies (GTAT) failed to reach performance targets in their contract with Apple because Apple kept changing the specifications? The 578 MUSD contract quickly devolved. Apple decided to withhold payment, and GTAT was running low on cash because they had spent their time and money adjusting to Apple's every whim, so the COO sold millions of dollars worth of stock. The company then declared bankruptcy, and the case went to court.

To quote GTAT's legal team, "Our management foolishly accepted oppressive and burdensome terms and obligations - so now we are trying the Chapter 11 route to escape the noose we placed around our own necks." But was it all GTAT's fault? We suggest perhaps the main contributor of the downfall was the use of the wrong contract type. A different type of contract, one based on the relationship and not the transaction, surely would have guided them to a better resolution long before things went south.

In complex deals with a lot of money at stake, the transactional contract is often too limited to do a good job in expectations management.

Yet despite the fact that there are limitations with transactional contracts, it is by far the most used contract model used today. We suggest organizations consider making the shift a formal relational contract. While not widely used in practice today, formal relational contracts are growing more popular around the world as megadealers find they are much more flexible and fit for purpose for the most large and complex deals.

The best way to understand what differentiates transactional and relational contracts is to compare five different aspects: focus, type of relationship, social norms, risk mitigation and completeness. The differences are illustrated below:

UNPACKING RELATIONAL CONTRACTING

	TRANSACTIONAL		RELATIONAL
DIMENSION	**TRANSACTIONAL CONTRACT**		**RELATIONAL CONTRACT**
FOCUS	The commercial transaction	→	The commercial relationship
RELATIONSHIP	Arm's-length relationship	→	Partnership
SOCIAL NORMS	Disconnected from social norms	→	Mutually discovered and agreed social norms
PRIMARY RISK MITIGATION MECHANISMS	Risk mitigation by use of market and state power	→	Risk mitigation and avoidance by continuous alignment of interest
PLANNING	Aims for completeness, i.e., tries to have contract clauses that cover all future events in the relationship	→	Accepts that complete planning is impossible and aims to create a fair and flexible framework for managing risk

1. Focus

In the transactional contract, the focus is on the *transaction*. In the relational contract, the focus is on the *relationship*.

Transactional contracts focus on what goods or services will be provided, the quality and the price. Think of a typical press release announcing a megadeal: "Buying Company has entered into a 1 billion USD deal with Selling Company over a five-year period, under which Selling Company will provide x, y and z." How do the parties arrive at the 1 billion USD figure? You might expect 1 billion USD to be paid upfront by the buyer, whereafter the seller would manufacture the products, provide the services and so on. But most of the time that doesn't happen. Instead, that money is paid over time, as the products or services are delivered. The 1 billion USD figure in the press release is a projection of the future value of all the exchanges of products or services that the parties, at the signing date, believe will be carried out during the contract term.

Sometimes it makes sense to focus on the transaction because the projections made in such press releases are realistic. But in many cases, what is contracted for is not what is actually needed. At some point the parties realize there is a need for additional services, increased or decreased scope, or that market circumstances have changed, etc. The projection made in the press release is often an illusion.

What does remain constant during the contract term is, however, the *relationship*. In the relational contract, the focus is on how the parties will manage their relationship, what their joint goals and objectives are, what standards they will act by, how they will govern changes of people, changes to the contract, innovation processes and so on. And since all successful commercial relationships are to a large extent based on trust, trust will be an important theme in the contracting process.

As a rule of thumb, a relational contract is best suited for megadeals that are dynamic in nature, where the parties cannot "nail the deal" at the signing date.

2. Type of relationship

In a transactional contract the parties establish an *arm's-length* relationship. This is the most common kind of commercial relationship, where the parties act as separate entities and don't feel obliged to look out for each other's interests. If, say, the seller has made a mistake in the price quote, has run into staffing trouble or some other problems, this is the seller's problem and the buyer does not have to take this into consideration. And vice versa. If the buyer has made a mistake in what products or services it actually needs or how it calculated its savings potential, this is the buyer's problem and not something the seller needs to bother with.

In contrast, a relational contract establishes a *partnership* between the parties.

There are many characteristics of a partnership, one main one being that the parties have obligations to look out for each other's interests - something that is lacking in a transactional contract. This means not only that the parties refrain from doing things that hurt each other, but also that they look out for each other's interests - regardless of whether they are obliged to do so in the contract or not. A good example of a relational contract in practice is the Swedish telco Telia. Telia has a complex web of over 16,000 sites that require facilities management and maintenance. Telia realized that it's transaction approach of working with 20 approved suppliers was not resulting in operational efficiencies or motivating suppliers to invest in best practices and innovations. Telia decided to do a Request for Partner which resulted in one supplier - Veolia - with which they created a formal relational contract.

A relational contract should also reflect reality when it comes to dependency. In some deals, the parties are actually autonomous and independent of one another. But in others there is a high level of dependency - such as with Telia when they shifted to one supplier.

Dependency is best tested by asking how much it would cost to leave

> **“ AS COMPANIES GROW FROM 100 MILLION USD TO 1 BILLION USD, THEY ARE INCREASINGLY LIKELY TO HAVE MUTUALLY DEPENDENT RELATIONSHIPS.”**

the relationship. Where switching costs are low, the parties are typically independent and it therefore often makes sense to have an arm's-length relationship.

In most megadeals, the parties are highly dependent. In 2017 the National Center for the Mid-Market found a high correlation between growth, size, and mutual dependence. As mid-market companies grow from 100 million USD to 1 billion USD, they are increasingly likely to have mutually dependent relationships. Because of this, switching costs can be high. For example, they may have integrated IT systems; built plants close to each other to lower logistics costs; or made other similar investments. In such cases, it is myopic to enter into a contract that pretends that the parties can act at arm's-length, without regard for each other's interests.

As a rule of thumb, a relational contract is best suited for deals where the parties are more dependent on each other.

3. Social norms

In the transactional contract, social norms are typically absent. In a relational contract, they constitute the foundation for the entire relationship.

A social norm is a standard of behavior. Some common social norms are honesty (telling the truth) and reciprocity (returning favors in kind). Social science has proven a clear tie between social norms and the effectiveness of a society or group of individuals.

A key difference between a transactional contract and a relational contract is how the parties use and formally embed social norms, not only in relationship, but also in the contract itself.

In a transactional contract, however, social norms play a small role - primarily because the parties operate in an arm's-length relationship. Under the transactional contract, it is generally accepted to treat the other party in ways that would be unacceptable in a friendship or family relationship. It is OK to lie, or at least not to tell the whole truth. It is OK to exercise power over the other party to gain benefits. There is no obligation to return favors in kind and so on. At best, a transactional contract might have a simple "good faith" clause.

In the relational contract, the parties deliberately embed social norms (referred to as Guiding Principles) into the contract. There are six Guiding Principles: reciprocity, autonomy, honesty, loyalty, equity and integrity. These principles serve as a foundation for negotiations, should be reflected in the contractual clauses, and guide the parties when they review changes to the contract.

4. Risk mitigation

As noted previously, a key function of any contract is to protect against the other party's opportunistic behavior. In the transactional contract, risks are mitigated through state and market power. In the relational contract, risks are mainly mitigated through continuous alignment of interests and expectations. Let's explore each.

In the transactional contract, risks are typically mitigated by threat of force or power. First, there is *state power*. This simply means that the contract is enforceable in court. The buyer says to the seller: if you don't do this or do that, I will take you to court. And vice versa. The threat of being taken to court provides incentives to comply with the contract. Second, there is *market power*. This means that each party can induce the other party to act in their interest by threatening to leave the relationship and go to someone else in the market. In many contracts, it is common for buyers to include a right to terminate, even if the seller has not breached the contract. This is called a termination for convenience right.

Mitigating risk in a transactional contract through state and market power can be very efficient. But often, these mechanisms can be inefficient and weak. For example, only in extreme cases does a buyer or seller take the other party to court. Litigation is often risky and expensive and hurts the relationship. If the parties have high dependency, i.e., if the costs of switching to another contracting party are high, the threat of market power is often equally weak. In many megadeals, which are often characterized by high complexity and dependency between the parties, using market and state power as risk mitigation can give a false sense of security.

> **"IN MEGADEALS, WHICH ARE OFTEN CHARACTERIZED BY HIGH COMPLEXITY AND DEPENDENCY, USING MARKET AND STATE POWER AS RISK MITIGATION CAN GIVE A FALSE SENSE OF SECURITY."**

In a relational contract, instead of having power as the main risk mitigation mechanism, the contract aims to create *continuous alignment of interests* between the parties. It would be naive to think the parties can maintain total alignment of interests and expectations at all times during the life of the relationship. But a great deal can be made to accomplish high alignment by formally embedding mechanisms to manage expectations continuously during the term of the contract.

For starters, the parties should agree on a shared vision and shared goals and objectives for their partnership, creating significant alignment during the earliest stages of the deal-making process. This shared vision and the Guiding Principles discussed above are combined into a formal statement of intent, which is embedded front and center in the Master Agreement. This statement of intent fulfills a critical function of aligning interests. In addition, the parties can use pricing models that align interests, for example by tying the seller's margin to the meeting of predefined goals and objectives of the buyer. One of the most important alignment mechanisms in a relational contract is the formal inclusion of clear structures and processes for relationship management – or governance. Relational contracts also use a formal mechanism for monitoring, managing and mitigating risks in a contract (instead of simply trying to shift risk through contractual clauses).

The potential gains of a contract structured in this way cannot be understated. As part of their effort to drive collaboration, FFG Enterprise put a simple but effective relational contract in place. This joint venture between the Royal Australian Navy, Defence Industry, and the Capability, Acquisition and Sustainment Group (CASG) established a mission to "deliver materially seaworthy guided missile frigates on time, every time."

After only 18 months, Capt. Greg Laxton, FFGSPO Director, FFG Enterprise Chairman, said they "achieved cultural and relational dividends, a significant reduction in sustainment costs, and a marked increase in the availability of Australia's primary naval air warfare asset to conduct operations." The results included a 44% decrease in labor costs per hour, a 38% decrease in defect incidence, and 100% on-time delivery.

As the example above shows, relational contracts are ideal for megadeals, where relationships have a high degree of dependency and potential for risk. Why? High dependency can strongly affect the efficiency of state or market power. And when there is a high degree of risk, it makes more sense to tackle the root cause by aligning interests and collaborating to achieve greater success rather than upholding a transaction by force.

5. Completeness

A transactional contract aims to be complete (i.e., address all things that can and will happen during the contract term), while a relational contract aims to be a flexible framework.

All contracts are incomplete. In simple deals, the holes and gaps in the contract tend to be small and few; thus a transactional contract does a good job. If we think about the second main function of the contract – expectations management – a transactional contract is perhaps ideal because it aims to have all expectations clearly spelled out prior to contract signing.

But as complexity and the likelihood of changes increase, the more illusory a complete contract becomes. As the number of clauses grows, it becomes harder and harder to actually understand the contract and for it to explicitly set out the expectations of the parties. And because transactional contracts involve arm's-length relationships, opportunistic behavior can flourish.

The relational contract is different. It accepts the fact that contracts are unavoidably incomplete. It aims instead to be more like a flexible framework than a complete projection of the future. The framework is provided by the adopted shared vision, strategic objectives, guiding principles and other more general mechanisms. The flexibility is provided by strong governance mechanisms to monitor the relationship and help the parties adapt to changing needs and circumstances during the contract term, based on the need to keep interests continuously aligned.

There is a challenge here from an expectations management viewpoint. The less complete the signed contract is, the more room there is for disagreement and different interpretations as to what to expect from one another. But this does not change the fact that the alternative - to aim for completeness - is worse in many deals with high complexity. A contract that is too complex and extensive will also fail to provide clear expectations. Striking the right balance between rigidity and flexibility in the contract is more of an art than a science and needs to be carefully dealt with in each relational contract. The solution is to be explicit about the realistic level of expectations. Sometimes, the parties can be explicit and detailed, but sometimes they must accept that expectations are tied to high-level outcomes and fair behavior according to the adopted guiding principles.

As a rule of thumb, a relational contract is best suited for megadeals where there is a high degree of complexity and where it is unrealistic or too difficult to write an almost complete contract.

Choosing the right contract form

In the previous section we shared some general rules of thumb for using a relational contract. When choosing which contract form is the best fit for your megadeal, you should analyze the deal according to the dimensions of *dependency* and *risk*.

As we saw above, the level of dependency between the parties - often best assessed through switching costs - is highly important. Where the level of dependency is low, it can make sense to use a transactional contract that establishes an arm's-length relationship, disregards social norms, mitigates risk through power, and aims to be complete. But if there is a medium to high level of dependency, the relational contract is the better choice.

When it comes to risk, we specifically want to point out the risk of conflicts of interests between the parties during the contract term. The potential for a conflict of interest almost always increases with the complexity and size of the deal. Transactional contracts are often a good fit for low-risk deals because state and market power risk-mitigation mechanisms can do a fairly good job. But as risk increases, power-based mechanisms become weak, and you will be best served with relational contracting mechanisms that focus on helping keep the parties continuously aligned throughout the life of the contract.

The choice of a transactional versus a relational contract is a critical one. It will affect the success of the entire deal. As such, the analysis of dependency and risk should not be taken lightly.

The contracting process

In the previous section we discussed the differences in the content between a transactional contract and relational contract. In this section we explore the differences in the contracting *process*.

There is not *one* standard process for entering into transactional contracts - but there are common practices.

One common practice is for business professionals to negotiate a deal, which is then followed by contracting phase. Often, a sales team from the seller side carries out the business negotiation, often with the procurement department or business units from the client side. Then, when this team thinks that most details of the deal have been nailed down, lawyers are brought in to start contract negotiations.

Having two separate negotiation processes is quite strange when you consider clauses such as limitation of liability. In which of the two processes should the limitations of liability of the parties be negotiated and decided? For many lawyers, this is a purely commercial matter. The limitation of liability is, so to say, the ultimate risk allocator in the deal. Above the liability cap, the damaged party will carry all risks. Since risk is something that, at least in theory, should be reflected in the price, many lawyers assume that the business negotiation team has made assumptions about broad risk allocation when negotiating the price. So the contract negotiation team will want to toss this question over the fence to the business negotiation team.

However, business negotiation teams rarely think about the limitation of liability; rather, they think liability is a matter for the lawyers and the contract negotiation team to solve – viewing it as a contractual rather than a commercial concern. So they toss the question back to the contract negotiation team.

The point here is not that one of the teams is wrong about where the limitation of liability negotiation belongs. The problem is the separation of commercial and contractual matters in the deal. This separation is illogical. All contractual matters are also commercial matters.

A second common practice in the transactional contract process is that the people making the deal don't typically stay behind and "live the deal." For example, on the seller side, it is common that a sales team, supported by one or more lawyers, conducts the contract negotiation. After the contract signing they go their own ways - throwing the contract over the fence for the delivery organization with a more or less good handover. Likewise, on the buyer side the procurement department can play a leading role in crafting the deal only to hand over the contract to the business unit receiving the services.

While the division of labor makes sense in small deals (where sales and procurement are involved in dozens if not hundreds of deals), this is bad practice for megadeals where a relationship of trust and transparency between people in both organizations is a critical element. But if the people expected to have this relationship during the contract term are not present in the negotiations, this will be hard to achieve.

Megadealers choosing a relational contract must therefore be careful about how the contracting process is carried out, since the wrong approach can lead to problematic situations where the parties expect a trustful partnership to be built, but where the process leads them to a traditional, arm's-length relationship. In the next section, we lay out a five-step approach to building a relational contract that incorporates both the process and content needed to create a successful relational contract.

We offer one word of caution for megadealers wanting to explore relational contracts: experience shows any attempt to enter into a relational contract using the traditional contracting process almost always fails or faces significant setbacks.

Five-step process for creating a relational contract

As outlined above, there are five essential dimensions for developing a relational contract. In this section, we build these into a five-step process.

1. *Focus on the relationship, not the deal.* This step helps you build the trust necessary to focus on the relationship. It includes ensuring alignment within your own organization and using a process for choosing a partner that considers relational competencies in addition to service offerings, quality levels, etc.
2. *Establish a partnership instead of an arm's-length relationship.* This step explores and lays the foundation of trust, transparency and compatibility between the parties that is required for a successful partnership.
3. *Embed social norms in the relationship.* This step helps the parties jointly discover and formally agree to the six guiding principles (social norms) of the relational contract.
4. *Avoid and mitigate risks through alignment of interests.* This step is designed to lay the foundation for continuously aligned interests. It starts with the parties agreeing upon a shared vision and strategic objectives for the partnership, specifying what joint success and value look like. Also ensuring that the pricing arrangement and contractual clauses later agreed upon support achievement of the vision and objectives.
5. *Create a fair and flexible framework.* This step establishes a robust governance framework for continuous relationship management. The parties agree upon the written contract clauses to establish the more specific rules of the relationship, all aligned with the six guiding principles.

Each step is explained in more detail.

Step 1: Focus on the relationship, not the deal

Focusing on the relationship instead of the deal has important consequences for both the contracting process and the actual content of the contract. At this stage, an organization entering into a megadeal must seek to create trust and consciously work to create a strong relationship between the parties.

An experienced megadealer (or one who is familiar with the five cornerstones outlined in this book) has already done a thorough job of mapping the ecosystem in the early stages of the deal. You will already know who the key stakeholders are, from top management to external advisors, procurement and sales managers. And if you did the work of achieving consensus, you will have ensured alignment before you enter the contracting process.

However, as megadealers are not usually involved in "living the deal," this can be a liability when it comes time to write the contract. The relational contracting process addresses this weakness head on by consciously including the people who will live the deal in the process. This enables the parties to begin building the relationship from the outset. It also fosters trust because the people who will deliver the deal are also the ones making contractual commitments. Trust is generated through alignment between words and actions, and in the words of one senior leader, "I knew we were going to be successful because I could look everyone in the eye and know I was making a commitment with the person I was going to be working with long after the ink was dry on the contract."

But trust is not only conveyed by and to individuals. There is such a thing as organizational trust and *organizational integrity*. To build trust, the organization must speak with one voice. But since every organization is made of individuals, it is critical to identify all stakeholders within your own organization early who may affect the trust level in the relationship you are about to enter into. The relational contracting process uses a cross-functional, team-based approach that ensures alignment both within organizations and across the contracting parties. Because decisions are made as a group, the parties achieve alignment of goals and objectives among those stakeholders, laying the foundation and implementing the relational tenet of mutual objectives later on.

Step 2: Establish a partnership

The second step in the relational contracting process is to consciously seek to establish the relationship. This starts early in the deal-making phase.

In most situations, contract negotiations are preceded by a competitive bidding process which is almost always focused on getting the best value for money. The three most common bidding processes are:

- Request for quote/price (RFQ) - designed to select a supplier based on a quoted price.
- Request for Proposal (RFP) - used to seek a more detailed proposal from potential suppliers beyond price, and which differentiates them based on how they will meet certain specifications.
- Request for Solution (RFS) - used when an organization does not know the best way to achieve specific business needs. Instead of stating specifications, the buyer instead states their needs and objectives, leaving to the supplier to propose a solution.

In all cases, the focus is typically on the transaction, not the relationship. It's about picking a supplier to meet a need - not about picking a potential partner.

More strategic relationships should use what is referred to as a Request for Partner process. Such a process helps an organization find a business partner with not only the right capabilities, but also the right "fit" for the relationship. Though unusual, when Swedish telecom company Telia decided to streamline the maintenance of their 16,000 technical sites across the country, that's exactly what they did. The RFP generated proposals from 20 different suppliers, and eventually resulted in a relational contract with Veolia. We detailed the process and outcomes in an extensive case study, which we now use as part of the Vested curriculum.

Not all organizations are ready to become a partner. And not all

> **NOT ALL ORGANIZATIONS ARE READY TO BECOME A PARTNER."**

organizations are a good fit with one another, depending on corporate cultures and other factors. A partnership is a relationship where the buyer and seller have a serious concern for the interests and success of one another, in which they genuinely look out for each other's interests, knowing that what is good for one of them is often good for both. As a megadealer you will already have a good understanding of whether or not the parties' foundation is strong enough to build a partnership.

Trust is a critical success factor in all relationships. However, trust does not exist at the start of a new relationship. Trust must be consciously built - and the relational contract is a fundamental building block. *Trust* must be combined with *high transparency* and *compatibility*.

Having the right stakeholders is ensured in the first step of the process. The next step is therefore to explore whether the parties are ready to build a relational contract, focusing on trust, transparency and compatibility.

This can be done by sitting down and asking some serious and uncomfortable questions:

1. Are we trustworthy? Do we align our actions with what we say?
2. Are we prepared to work collaboratively and in good faith with our partner, or do we feel we must use power to induce them to do as we want?
3. Is there evidence that our potential partner(s) shares our values and readiness to operate under shared principles?
4. Are we both prepared to be transparent, i.e., to share information about our plans for the future, our internal challenges, our risk register, our costs and even margins?
5. Are we compatible? Do we share a base of organizational values, interests and views of the world? Is this alignment likely to continue?
6. Do we have evidence to support our answers, or are we just hoping?

Step 3: Embed social norms in the relationship

The third step in the relational contracting process is to actively embed social norms into the relationship. Let's compare this to contracting for a transactional contract.

When the ink has dried on a transactional contract, all the rights and obligations of the parties can be read in the written document. If the written document is silent and neither party can prove there is some verbal agreement, no rights or obligations exist. Opportunism can flourish.

But society outside a commercial environment is different. In society, people have moral obligations toward each other. These moral obligations impact behaviors, feelings and actions. Take the norm of *honesty*. If someone lies to you and you discover it, that person will feel ashamed - a symptom of the breach of a social norm. You may avoid that person, creating a pattern of passive-aggressive behaviors and actions.

Or take for instance the *norm of reciprocity*, which creates an obligation to return in kind. If friends invite you to dinner, you will feel obliged to reciprocate and invite them for dinner or do some other favor for them (bring flowers and wine or offer to take them sailing on your boat). If you don't reciprocate, you most likely will feel ashamed. Your friends may blow off your actions as forgetfulness. But over time, if you do not reciprocate, they will quit investing in the relationship and stop inviting you to dinner because they will not feel their actions are valued.

The relational contracting process formally embeds six guiding principles into the relationship – and the contract itself. Although principles can be added to this list, these six are based on scientific research in psychological, social and economic theory:

1. The principle of *reciprocity* - the principle obliges the parties to return in kind.
2. The principle of *autonomy* - the principles obliges the parties to abstain from using power, allowing each party to make autonomous decisions, independent of undue influence from one another.
3. The principle of *honesty* - the principle obliges the parties to tell the truth about facts and their intentions.

4. The principle of *loyalty* - the principle obliges the parties to look out for each other's interests and treat them with equal value. This means, amongst other things, that risks and costs must be allocated to keep them low in the partnership.
5. The principle of *equity* - the principle obliges the parties to keep proportionality in the contract, for example between risk and potential rewards.
6. The principle of *integrity* - the principle obliges the parties to be consistent over time, i.e., to treat like cases alike and to avoid opportunistic behavior but to always, when in doubt, act in accordance with the other guiding principles.

What would happen if you tried to establish a partnership and took one of these principles away? Would a partnership without honesty and loyalty survive for long? A relationship without equitable allocation of risks and costs would soon deteriorate, as would a relationship which, in breach of the integrity principle, is not consistent over time in applying the other principles.

The guiding principles fulfill at least four important functions in the relational contract:

1. They will guide the parties during the rest of the negotiations. The only valid arguments in the discussions are those than can be justified under one or more of the guiding principles.
2. All the contract clauses should be aligned to the principles. This will, as far as possible, ensure that the contract is fair and balanced, and facilitate the creation of a frictionless relationship.
3. The guiding principles should, with a shared vision, constitute the basis for interpreting the agreement, both when the written clauses are ambiguous and when the contract is silent on a particular matter. We will deal with this further in the next section.
4. The guiding principles also assist the parties when changing the contract.

Not only do the guiding principles ensure a fair and balanced agreement, they also ensure the contract remains mutually beneficial throughout its term. To use power will be a breach of contract because of the agreed-upon principle of autonomy, so when dealing with change, the parties must find solutions sanctioned by the principles of loyalty and equity. Any solution that harms one party more than it is beneficial to the other party will be in breach of the principle of loyalty, and the principle of equity will ensure avoidance of opportunistic risk transfer to the other party. As we will see in the next section, the guiding principles are therefore also a key instrument for risk avoidance and mitigation.

By embedding the guiding principles into the relationship, the parties also lay the foundation for implementing the relational tenets of risk allocation, communication, pain and gain sharing and no-blame culture, to be formalized in the fourth and fifth steps of the relational contracting process.

Will the guiding principles create a failsafe system? No, but they will create a system much better suited to keeping interests aligned than with transactional contracts, which only deal with conflicts of interests as a fact that cannot be avoided.

To a greater or lesser extent, the guiding principles exist in most relationships. However, because they are rarely stated and openly discussed, we are often unaware of their presence. Often, we deliberately (or subconsciously) ignore them in search for short-term advantages. The first step is, therefore, to have an open and candid discussion to define the guiding principles. As social norms, they exist between the parties before the discussions start, so they are not invented. For most, it will be the first time the parties (or even individuals) have openly discussed how to apply social norms in a business context – let alone a contract.

The six guiding principles are best codified in a charter to the relational contract - preferably right up front. Some organizations put this in the main body of the contract while others create a schedule (often the first schedule) outlining how the parties will behave over the life of their relationship.

Step 4: Avoid and mitigate risks through alignment of interests

As we have seen above, a transactional contract mitigates risk through a combination of market and state power. The conflicting interests are accepted and their symptoms attacked. Even if the parties do share goals and objectives to some extent, they rarely have any obligations to look out for each other's interests when goal conflicts arise.

In the relational contract, you take a different approach: you attack the causes of conflicting interests and not their symptoms. The intention is to always keep interests aligned. Misaligned interests are the most common cause of value leakage and unnecessary transaction costs. *It is only when the parties' interests are misaligned that opportunism becomes a problem in a commercial relationship.* The source of misaligned interests is *conflicting goals and objectives*. If a client's goals and objectives can only be achieved at the cost of a supplier achieving their goals and objectives, interests will be misaligned and opportunism and friction will follow. For example, a common source of value leakage is when the client's goal of lowering costs comes into conflict with the supplier's goals of increasing revenue and margin. This is not a goal conflict by

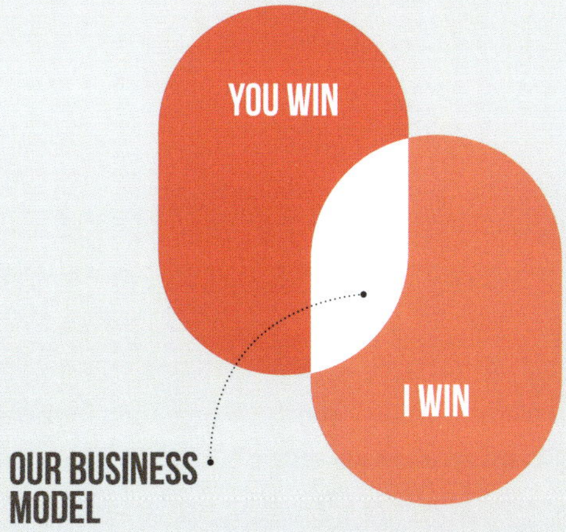

> **LOYALTY REQUIRES THAT EACH PARTY'S INTERESTS ARE TREATED WITH EQUAL VALUE."**

nature, but instead a result of conventional economic models.

A relational contract - by design - seeks to align interests by avoiding goal conflicts between the parties. Joint - not separate - goals and objectives should be adopted. Doing this is a logical consequence of the two parties having agreed to the guiding principle of loyalty. Loyalty requires that each party's interests are treated with equal value. Building conflicting interests into the relationship would breach loyalty, since it would mean that one party's interests would be considered less valuable.

There are three main components in a relational contract aimed at mitigating and avoiding risk through aligned interests:

1. The six guiding principles
2. A shared vision and a set of common strategic objectives for the partnership
3. A governance process for continuous risk and change management

Here we will focus on the shared vision and strategic objectives and the importance of finding the right economic model for the partnership.

To adopt a shared vision and strategic objectives is to adopt a common view of what is valuable. An individual's and an organization's interests are tied to what they perceive as valuable. In the market, what is valuable is most often tied to goals and objectives that, when achieved, generate revenue or improve productivity. For public and non-profit organizations, what is valuable is often tied to the task or function to be fulfilled, for example providing health care, infrastructure or education.

A shared vision for the partnership can be created based on what the parties perceive is valuable. This is a powerful exercise and should always be done jointly. An effective method is to let everyone in the room think about a few words they want to be included, words like "together," "customer satisfaction," "empower" and "world-class quality." Everyone in the group then can assign three votes to what the group has come up with, indicating a direction for the continued work. After this, the parties can draft statements, which, step-by-step, are merged into a view of a bright future - the shared vision. A good shared vision should not be too long. It should paint a successful common future and be aligned with both parties' business strategies. You know you have a good shared vision when everyone in the room smiles, feels engaged and wants to roll up their sleeves immediately to achieve the vision. For example, Vancouver Coastal Health and its strategic partner for environmental services created this shared vision:

> *Patient and Resident focused Environmental Services of the highest quality and reliability. Our commitment to collaboration, innovation, and shared governance will drive value and create an exceptional healthcare environment for all.*

The process for getting to a first draft can be done quickly, but we advise that the parties then take a day or two to reflect, allowing them to "socialize" the draft. This will allow for insights and thoughts about changes or adjustments. It will also prevent the urge to spend hours wordsmithing.

When you have created a shared vision, it is often a good idea to break it down into several shared objectives, which specify in more detail what the shared vision means. The objectives are based on the intent of the relationship. Objectives typically fall into one of three categories:

- Outcome-based - which are boundary-spanning business transformation outcomes that typically can only be achieved with a high degree of collaboration (e.g., the mountain climber cannot get to the top of Mount Everest without the Sherpa).
- Output-based - which are typically tied to a specific scope of one or both parties (e.g., service level agreements tied to a supplier's work scope).
- Transactional - which are typically linked to the effectiveness of a task or activity.

In a relational contract, the objectives should typically be outcome-based or output-based. As in the case of the Australian Royal Navy's joint venture, mentioned above, common objectives can be to increase customer satisfaction, lower total cost of ownership, gain market share, avoid business interruptions, etc. We advise using a maximum of 4-6 objectives, otherwise the parties will lose focus governing the relationship.

The steps above will typically not be enough to align interests. It is usually also necessary for the parties to take a hard look at how risks will be allocated and at the economics of the deal, as both can create perverse incentives due to conflicting interests. Each of these is discussed in more detail.

We'll first look at risk allocation. Risk should be allocated following the guiding principles, which would have been agreed to and adopted. Understand the role of the guiding principles in avoiding and mitigating risks in the partnership. The guiding principles will not only guide the relational contract process and negotiation; they will also have hard consequences for the contract content.

No matter how perfect your objectives and planning are at the onset of the contract, all contracts are incomplete. Conflicts of interests will arise anyway - as business happens, changes in the market occur and priorities shift. Your contract will be full of cracks and holes, with risks and events not dealt with in the contract clauses. When this happens, go back to your shared vision and guiding principles. Why? The shared vision and guiding principles fulfill an important role in dealing with the tricky combination of arising conflicts of interests in an incomplete contract. This is done by agreeing on how the contract should be interpreted when something is ambiguous or even silent in the contract.

How to interpret contracts is an important part of contract law in most jurisdictions. But the legal rules and principles for this vary significantly. In Common Law countries, the four corner of the document principle is a key component, even though the principle today has so many exceptions that its continued applicability can be questioned. In other legal traditions, for example in civil law countries, more attention is paid to the intentions of the parties at the time of signing the contract.

In a relational contract, the parties should contractually agree that the contract clauses will be interpreted in the light of the shared vision and guiding principles. They should clearly agree that the shared vision and principles shall, so to say, fill in the blanks when the contract is silent on which rights and obligations the parties have in a particular situation. For some, this may seem to be a controversial move to make. To say that the shared vision and guiding principles shall apply when the contract is silent means adding obligations where the contractual language in the contract is silent or uncertain. For a contract lawyer used to "Entire Agreement" clauses where the goal is to ensure contract obligations are exhausted by the written word, this will seem risky. This perception is, however, based on the incorrect transactional contract assumptions that contracts can and should be complete. As we have seen, this is an illusion. All complex contracts are incomplete and unless the cracks and holes are dealt with through the shared vision and guiding principles, opportunism will enter and value will erode. Ensuring that the contract is interpreted according to the shared vision and guiding principles therefore decreases the risk of the relationship significantly. Remember also Dworkin's description of a society of principles shared above; a partnership contains rights and obligations broader than the written word.

The second key consideration comes in structuring the economics of the relationship. It would be naive to think that money doesn't matter. It is important to understand the context of an economic model as it relates to a relational contract. To be clear, the economic model of the relationship - how the parties generate and allocate value between themselves - is *not* an integral part of the relational contract. Different economic models can be used in a relational contract. Rather, the economic model is a component of the relational contract. Think of the relational contract as setting the *rules of the game* for the relationship and the economic model as establishing the stakes of this game.

The economic model can in many deals create either aligned or conflicting interests. When they are conflicting, it will undermine the relational contract's purpose to create continuous alignment of interests. The very process of creating the relational contract enables the parties to solve the often toughest part of any commercial negotiation - the price/value negotiation. Because of adopting the guiding principles, the parties will be both obliged and incentivized to find a model that, without usage of power, respects loyalty and equity, i.e., that treats both parties' interests with equal value and applies proportion between risk and rewards. The important relational tenet of sharing of gains and pains should be implemented here. The economic models that can and should be used under different circumstances in primarily customer-supplier relationships is examined in the book *Strategic Sourcing in the New Economy*.

Step 5: Create a fair and flexible framework

As set out above, a relational contract accepts that complete planning is impossible. Instead, the contracting parties try to establish a fair *and* flexible framework for their deal and their relationship. The relational contract operates as a *framework*, setting forth clear rights and obligations as the parties pursue their shared vision and objectives. But on a more general level, a relational contract is designed for *flexibility*, enabling the parties to deal with change. This means creating a sound governance structure and mechanisms to help the parties manage the business in a dynamic environment, not just enabling the customer to manage the supplier. The guiding principle and relational tenets ensure that the explicitly laid out rights and obligations and the processes for managing the relationship are kept *fair* during the term of the contract.

The foundation of a relational contract is trust, but trust is a complex phenomenon. It should not be mistaken for naivety. We have noted how we humans have a tendency for opportunism, looking out for our own interests to the detriment of others. Evolution has made us that way and it would be naive to ignore this. And somewhat paradoxically, trust exists because of opportunism. To trust someone is to have confidence she will do what she says, *despite* her opportunistic DNA. Without opportunism, trust would serve no purpose.

But trust also exists because evolution simultaneously has made us into moral creatures with a strong sense of fairness. If we were *only* opportunistic, trust would serve no purpose. To trust someone is to have faith that a person's sense of fairness will be stronger than her tendency for opportunism.

So, trust rests on our combined and opposing tendencies for opportunism and sense of fairness given to us by millions of years of evolution. The aim of the relational contract is to create circumstances favorable for our sense of fairness to dominate over our opportunistic nature. But that does not mean this opportunistic nature is ignored.

At this stage of the process, three cornerstones of the framework are in place. These cornerstones are: the shared vision, the strategic objectives and the guiding principles. Here is how they work together.

- The shared vision and the objectives are set at the beginning of the relationship. They can be changed over time, but they should typically lay the foundation for the foreseeable duration of the contract.
- The guiding principles should be fixed and should be strictly adhered to, not only during the contracting process, but also post-contract signing.
- The parties should be flexible in the means they use to achieve the shared vision and objectives, as long as they always act in line with the guiding principles.

To create a fair and flexible framework based on the three cornerstones requires the parties to agree on clear rights and obligations regarding "the deal" and the risks related to it and the relationship. In addition, the parties must agree on a robust governance process for managing the relationship.

As set out above, the parties must agree on clear rights and obligations regarding the goods or services in the deal, their quality and timely delivery. The parties will also have to agree on the contract duration, payment terms, confidentiality, rules for terminating the contract, how to compensate each other if breaches occur, what limits should be set to the parties' liabilities, ownership of intellectual property, etc.

The trick is to find an appropriate level of detail to ensure that it is a *framework* and not a complete manual. The clauses you adopt in the contract will play a role in interpreting the contract. But the contact language you don't write will play an important role providing the flexibility you need to manage change in a dynamic business environment. The key is finding the right balance.

The guiding principles play a vital role in developing and interpreting the contractual clauses and language. First, the parties must ensure that all the written clauses are aligned with the guiding principles from the start. Second, the guiding principles provide a way of interpreting the clauses (and lack of contract language).

A quick look at a typical transactional contract shows that many of the typical clauses are in breach of the guiding principles. Some examples are:

- Non-reciprocal and non-equitable audit rights, indemnification rights or limitations of liability.
- Sweeper clauses obliging the supplier to provide services without a right to compensation under the equity principle.
- Termination for convenience clauses giving one party discretionary power in the relationship, in breach of the autonomy principle.
- Limitation of liability clauses that fail to keep the risks for the relationship low, breaching the loyalty principle.

The last remaining cornerstones of a relational contract create a structure and mechanisms for managing the relationship post-contract signing. This is often called governance and it is crucial to sustaining the relationship, ensuring continual alignment of interests and helping the parties to remain focused on the vision and objectives. Sound governance includes incorporating these seven mechanisms into how you will jointly manage the relationship post-contract signing:

1. *Create a tiered management structure.* The number of tiers can vary based on the scale and complexity of your relationship. The most common is a three-tier structure that enables the parties to focus at the operational, management, and strategic or executive levels.

2. *Establish clear roles.* Good governance ensures the parties to focus on managing for today (service/product delivery), managing for tomorrow (transformation and change management), managing the economics (commercial management) and managing the overall relationship. We recommend larger contracts not only clearly spell out the roles, but also establish separate roles for areas to enable proper focus. A separate transformation role is essential for large-scale outsourcing deals where transformation and innovation are essential.
3. *Establish peer-to-peer communications protocols.* To enable efficient and effective communication, the parties should shorten the communication lines and let the right people on each side connect and communicate directly and not via an account manager or contract manager.
4. *Develop a communications cadence.* To keep momentum in the relationship, the parties should agree a frequency for their meetings at operational, tactical and strategic level.
5. *Develop a process to maintain continuity.* A relationship is created by people and if people in the governance structure change, it is critical to have processes ensuring that new individuals are educated and taken on board to ensure continuity in the relationship. We recommend larger contracts establish "key man" provisions for both parties.
6. *Establish a performance management program.* The parties should agree on joint reports to continuously follow up their performance, i.e., their journey towards the shared vision and strategic objectives.
7. *Establish processes for risk management and contract changes.* The parties should agree on a process for reviewing whether the contract needs changes to ensure that the shared vision is met and the guiding principles are followed. As part of this, they should agree on a process to continuously identify, assess and deal with upcoming risks. If a need for change arises (i.e., identification of new risk or other factors), the parties should have a simple process for formaliz-

ing such changes and make them legally binding. All changes must be aligned to the adopted guiding principles.

Relational contracts - an ideal fit for megadeals

While transactional contracts may be acceptable in many situations, as we have tried to show, they are not fit for more strategic and complex commercial agreements. As business relationships evolve, so should the contracts that govern them. It is time to put past dogmas, policies and contract templates aside and embrace a new form of contracting as a way to actually drive business in the new economy. This does not mean transactional contracts should be abandoned, but rather they should be used only when they are a good fit.

A good way to think about which type of contracting is a good fit is to ask, "Is beef a commodity?" It might be to the local grocery retailer, but for McDonald's, beef is a strategic weapon and commands a highly strategic relationship with suppliers. A customer thinking about outsourcing will have a different perspective to a supplier trying to gain a competitive advantage. A government planning to build a hospital will have a different perspective to a technology company that wants to create a strategic alliance with companies in other markets. And so on.

However, given what everyone is trying to achieve with any contract – to make plans for the future while coping with our limited capabilities for planning and the tendency for opportunism – there are some common factors that will always point towards a relational contract as the optimal choice.

EXERCISE

Gather your team and evaluate how you could proceed with contracting according to the five-step process for creating a relational contract.

Examine your current contracts. How are they strong, where are they weak, and where could you improve? If your existing contracts are more transactional than relational, consider how having a relational contract might have affected changes or decisions that have taken place since the contract signing.

KEY TAKEAWAYS

1. As a megadealer, you play a key role in determining what type of contract is best suited for your deal. There are two basic forms of contracts: transactional contracts and relational contracts.
   A. When dependency, risk, and complexity are low, an arm's length transactional contract can generally be used since the risks of misaligned interests can be mitigated through market power.
   B. However, a relational contract is the recommended approach for more strategic deals being done in the new economy because a competitive advantage cannot usually be gained in an arm's length relationship, and misalignment of interests creates friction and high transaction costs.
2. Transactional and relational contracts primarily differ in five ways: in their focus, type of relationship, social norms, risk mitigation and completeness. Understanding the demands of your deal and the subsequent relationship can help determine the preferred contract type.
3. David Frydlinger and Kate Vitasek's five-step process for creating a relational contract includes:
   A. Focusing on the relationship, not the deal.
   B. Establishing a partnership instead of an arm's-length relationship.
   C. Embedding social norms in the relationship.
   D. Avoiding and mitigating risks through alignment of interests.
   E. Creating a fair and flexible framework.

AFTERWORD

WHAT'S NOT IN THIS BOOK?

In reality, a megadeal is a topic of enormous proportions. The business of many of the world's largest enterprises depends entirely on megadeals. Still, there are no other books than this one on the topic. We are very humble about the depth and breadth of the subject.

Although we have extensive knowledge about some of the topics below, and in reality could have put them in the book or written separate books for them, some require more research for us to write meaningfully about them.

The megadeal maturity model and the megadeal organization

Now you have read the book. If your team has decided that it's not going to be "shelf help" but rather self-help, there are a few real challenges ahead.

- How do you implement the megadeal model and where do you start?
- What are the risks?
- What should your megadeal organization look like?

Negotiation of megadeals

Negotiating a megadeal is different because of the need for transformation and risk on both the buying and selling side.

- How well equipped are your teams to deal with negotiating a megadeal?
- What are the costs of poor negotiation?
- What would the benefit be if you improved your negotiation skills by just 10%?

Procurement organizations for megadeal buyers

Companies approach procurement in very different ways, and their procurement organizations have different strengths compared to their functional areas. This will partly decide how your team will approach the sales and marketing of megadeals.

- Are you conscious about your megadeal strategy and prepared to adjust your approach depending on how the client's procurement is organized and how strong it is?
- Where do you perform best? When are you in deals oriented towards functional areas (the business) or when you are in deals where procurement is really strong?
- How important is it for you to improve your knowledge about how your clients' procurement organizations are set up?

Sales and marketing KPIs for megadeals

If you are a sales manager working with traditional or transactional selling, you probably work with leading indicators such as the number of meetings, proposals, etc. And if you're in SMB B2B marketing, maybe it is SQL or MQL, etc. Have you ever tried to get a megadealer to report the number of meetings she/he has on a consistent basis? Our guess is that you will have one very pissed off megadealer.

- Do you have great ways to measure sales and marketing for your megadeals?
- Do your ways of measurement actually work?
- What are the second-order consequences when you measure poorly?

In-depth megadeal lead generation, marketing, and branding

Account-based marketing, social selling and the fundamental messaging architecture are great tools and capabilities to master in your organization. As seasoned marketers, we also know that we can't cover everything with in-depth case studies, etc. Branding (barely covered at all) is also different, for example, because of the level of risk mitigation that is needed compared to traditional B2B sales. In a megadeal, it is critical that your brand is associated with low risk. Yet few organizations know how to measure the success of their branding efforts.

Are your lead generation, marketing and branding up to speed for megadeals?

- What needs to be improved?
- What are the positive effects of world-class lead generation, marketing, and branding?
- What are the second-order consequences of staying at your current state of lead generation, marketing, and branding?

Leadership for megadeals

Winning a megadeal is a team effort. There are no "lone wolf megadealers" because there is such a great need for coordination, change driving, consensus, etc. Strong leadership skills are essential. We would argue that there are also special leadership abilities that megadealers need to have or develop. One example is handling the complexity of the ecosystem.

- Do your megadealers have strong leadership skills?
- How are you performing in these areas and what needs to be improved?
- What is it costing you right now if you are not improving?

ACKNOWLEDGEMENTS

THANK YOU

We are both optimistic people, so when we decided to write a book over a cup of coffee, we could not imagine how this would end.

Because we both have backgrounds in sales and marketing, we were quickly up and running.

Name. Check.

Graphical identity. Check.

Website. Check.

The main scope of the book. Check.

Updated titles to include “author” on social media. Check.

After six months, we had the painful realization that there were still a few more checks to go.

This is where the magic accountability of public declarations kicked in. Quitting was not an option. Instead, we received great support from Tonya S. Pixton, PhD, our head of research, who spent nine months researching and interviewing megadealers full-time to isolate the ingredients in the secret sauce. After the bulk of the research was finished, we locked ourselves in a room and finished the core of the book.

To understand the level of sweat and hard work, it took us another 10 months to finish this first edition of the book, a task which would not have been possible without the great support of our editor, Cole Ruth.

Still, without the bright brains, and unconditional love and support of our significant others, there would be no *Megadeals* research project or book. Thank you, Anna Engman (Christopher's wife) and Tina Mitic (Johan's partner).

We also want to thank our awesome team: our art directors and graphic designers, Tomas Ring, Josefin Herolf, Frida Jansson and Lina Földessy; our proofreader, Paul Redstone; and our indefatigable project manager, Ulrika Carmine.

Last but not least, enormous thanks to all the contributors who have made this project possible, in particular: Alexander Helling, David Frydlinger and Kate Vitasek for their significant contributions on financing and contracting; Bora Brännström, David Klättborg and Mark Stouse, all of whom took the time to contribute their insights, and to read and provide feedback on the entire book; to Konrad Bergström, Johan Bjorklund, Nicky Briggs, Emelie Meurk Demerud, Tomas Eriksson, Alice Heiman, Pål Lind, Mark Ogne, Walt Parmer, Mikael Philipsson, Jonas Rutström, Matt Senatore, Sofia Svanholt, Navin Thukkaram, Sangram Vajre, Thomas Westin and Andreas Wikholm for sharing their stories in these pages and for taking the time to read and comment on specific chapters; and to the many megadealers who participated in our research, among them: Mike Adams, Marva Bailer, Valerie Bonebrake, Andrey Bozhenko, James Caton, Henry Choi, Stephanie Chung, Genevieve Dozier, Lars Eldh, Shari Elia, Petra Goude, Jitendra Hariramani, Ashley Healy, Alice Heiman, Ted Heiman, Hany Hussein, Thomas Klang, Olof, Lindberg, Janice Mars, Samantha McKenna, Mareo McCracken, Krista Moore, Megendran Naidoo, Martina Oppstedt, Carolyn Rehling, Lori Richardson, Kathryn Rose, Mehdi Sahel, Michael Sainburg, Dale Sands, Siddharth Sawkar, Brian Shultz, Sheeza Shakeel, Andreas Sjölund, Terry Stone, Robert Szczerba, Paul Thompson,

Erik Thornberg, Patrick Vloemans, Geert van de Wouw, Josephine Wang, Christer Westerberg, Jan Wäreby and Göran Åsen. Many more megadealers and megamarketers contributed along the way - in interesting or challenging discussions after our presentations and events, in initial research calls, at offices and around dinner tables: you know who you are. If your name is missing from these pages it's only due to the daunting process of keeping track of you all, not because your insights mattered less. We are so very grateful and lucky to have friends and colleagues like you.

Thank you all for supporting us in creating what we hope will be a megadeal of a book!

Johan Aberg & Christopher Engman

REFERENCES

This book draws on knowledge gleaned from many sources over the history of our careers.

Those we have quoted or mentioned by name in these pages include:

Introduction

1. Adapted from ProSales' Buying Logic Model by Henrik Larsson-Broman, Peter Siljerud, and Markus Ejenäs, "Supertrends - Future-proof Your Sales and Marketing" ProSales Institute (Stockholm, 2018).

Chapter 2

1. See James Moore, "Predators and Prey: A New Ecology of Competition," Harvard Business Review, hbr.org/1993/05/predators-and-prey-a-new-ecology-of-competition (last accessed on September 16, 2019).

2. See Ray Dalio, Principles: Life and Work
(New York, NY: Simon & Schuster, 2017).

Chapter 4

1. Rizan Flenner, "How to Identify and Nurture a Sales Champion," iSEEit (2016),
now.iseeit.com/how-to-identify-a-meddic-champion
(last accessed on September 16, 2019).
2. Jim Holden, The Selling Fox: A Field Guide for Dynamic Sales Performance
(Hoboken, NJ: Wiley, 2002).
3. Unknown author, "The Challenger Sales Guide to Engaging Mobilizers" Revegy
www.revegy.com/blog/challenger-sales-guide-engaging-mobilizers
(last accessed on September 16, 2019).

Chapter 5

1. Daniel Kahneman, Thinking, Fast and Slow
(New York, NY: Farrar, Straus and Giroux, 2013).
2. Claudia Hammond, Mind over Money: The Psychology of Money and How to Use It Better
(New York, NY: Harper Perennial, 2016).
3. Stephen M. R. Covey, The Speed of Trust:
The one thing that changes everything
(New York, NY: Free Press, 2006).
4. Sharon Begley, "Expectations May Alter Outcomes Far More Than We Realize" The Wall Street Journal (2003),
www.wsj.com/articles/SB106815408551985600
(last accessed on September 16, 2019).

Chapter 6

1. Brad McDonald, "Emotional Buying – You Can't Sell Without It" Sandler Training blog, www.sandler.com/blog/emotional-buying-you-cant-sell-without-it (last accessed on September 16, 2019).
2. Matthew Dixon and Brent Adamson, The Challenger Sale: Taking Control of the Customer Conversation (New York, NY: Portfolio/Penguin, 2011).

Chapter 7

1. Simon Sinek, Start with Why: How Great Leaders Inspire Everyone to Take Action (New York, NY: Portfolio/Penguin, 2009).

Chapter 9

1. Alex Mandossian, "Silent Assassin of Biz Growth" All Selling Aside, podcast episode 51, www.allsellingaside.com/2019/03/04/51-sloppy-success-is-better (last accessed on September 16, 2019).

Chapter 10

1. Wikipedia contributors, "List of business and finance abbreviations", Wikipedia, The Free Encyclopedia, en.wikipedia.org/wiki/List_of_business_and_finance_abbreviations (last accessed on January 2019).

Chapter 11

1. Wikipedia contributors, "Contract", Wikipedia, The Free Encyclopedia, en.wikipedia.org/w/index.php?title=Contract&oldid=915983287 (last accessed on September 16, 2019).
2. Compiled by the IACCM, "2018 Top Terms in Negotiation - Most Negotiated Terms and Conditions Research", available to IACCM members only at: www.iaccm.com/resources/?id=10243
3. Pierre Mitchell, "Could Proper Procurement Have Saved Apple and GT Advanced?" Spend Matters (2014), spendmatters.com/2014/10/29/could-proper-procurement-have-saved-apple-and-gt-advanced-a-cautionary-tale-of-the-wrong-type-of-source-to-settle (last accessed on September 16, 2019).
4. Kate Vitasek, "Relational Contracting On The Rise With The Success Of The Australian Navy," Forbes (2016), www.forbes.com/sites/katevitasek/2016/11/30/relational-contracting-on-the-rise-with-the-success-of-the-australian-navy/#d8f1aee303a3 (last accessed on September 16, 2019).
5. For more information on Vancouver Coastal Health's shared partner vision, see: Kate Vitasek, Jeanne King and Bonnie Keith, "From Competitive to Collaborative Bidding Approaches: How Vancouver Coastal Harnessed the Potential of Supplier Collaboration for Environmental Services" Vested for Success Case Study, available for download at: www.vestedway.com/vested-library